Under the Mountain

Under the Mountain

Molly Flagg Knudtsen

University of Nevada Press
Reno, Nevada
1982

University of Nevada Press, Reno, Nevada 89557 USA
© Molly Flagg Knudtsen 1982. All rights reserved
Designed by Sandra Mahan
Photographs by Jonas Dovydenas
Printed in the United States of America

Library of Congress Cataloging in Publication Data

Knudtsen, Molly Flagg.
  Under the mountain.

  1. Grass Valley (Lander County and Eureka County,
Nev.)—Social life and customs—Addresses, essays,
lectures. 2. Grass Valley (Lander County and Eureka
County, Nev.)—History—Addresses, essays, lectures,
3. Austin (Nev.)—Social life and customs—Addresses,
essays, lectures. 4. Austin (Nev.)—History—Addresses,
essays, lectures. 5. Knudtsen, Molly Flagg—Addresses,
essays, lectures. I. Title.
F847.G7K86   1982   979.3'33   82-8552
ISBN 0-87417-072-9   AACR2

"How to Bake Bread With a 'Green Jacket,
Red Cap, and White Owl's Feather' " is
reprinted from the October 1963 issue of
Family Circle Magazine. © 1963 The Family
Circle, Inc. All rights reserved.
  "The Never-Never Houses of Nevada" and
"The Stones of the Blue Sky Magic" were first
published in *Vogue.*
  "Double Trouble" and "A Day on the
Mountain with the Basque Buckaroos" first
appeared in *Nevada* magazine in the Spring
1966 and Fall 1966 issues, respectively.
  "Why I Stopped Riding Sidesaddle," "A
Flake of Flint, A Sherd of Earthenware," and
"Chrysanthemums Among the Sage" are
published here for the first time.
  The remaining pieces in this volume first
appeared in the *Reese River Reveille,* Austin,
Nevada.

CONTENTS

PREFACE

ON A STILL DAY in January you can hear the mountain talking to itself. Rumbling. Grumbling. The sound comes from deep in its huge body. Mount Callaghan is an old mountain. It mourns aloud, like an old man, for the days of its youth, when rocks danced in the sky and the world was a wonder of fire and ice. All that has come after is only erosion.

Time has left the mountain bald, stoop-shouldered, dying down eternity. The glacial snows have melted, leaving great scars along its flanks. The warm waters have receded until only the fossilized starfish remain.

White clouds cap the top of the mountain, extending soft fingers down canyons and ridges. Wild storms scream through the passes, rage into the long valley, flattening the quaking aspens and twisting the trunks of the mahogany trees.

In summer the sun sinks late in the cleft of Skull Creek Pass. In winter it veers south behind Callaghan Canyon. Summer solstice. Winter solstice. The rock cairns on the peaks mark the year's passage.

Mount Callaghan lies like a giant hand on my life. From the day I came to live under its shadow in Grass Valley, I have felt its terrible strength; sustaining, restraining.

"Where do you live?" they ask.

What else can I say but, "I live under the mountain. . . ."

INTRODUCTION
The Vanishing World of Central Nevada

WHEN I WAS GROWING UP the sun never set on the British Empire. What a wonderfully well-ordered world it was, with five o'clock tea every afternoon, devoted and autocratic servants, God in his Anglican heaven, and everyone else from sea to shining sea wishing they too could be English.

Of course, I wasn't really English. I was American. But after years at Miss Spaulding's finishing school, presentation at Court, some brisk grooming by genuinely English relatives, a London Season, and several years at the University of London, I could pass for the genuine article even though my family on both sides had lived for generations in America.

My father, Montague Flagg, had died when I was very young. His family, though tainted with artistic tendencies, was impeccably English, and Uncle Ernest Flagg wrote a *History of New England* which was quite simply a history of the Flagg family and their many relatives.

My mother's family was, if possible, even more English. Arthur Benson owned the seaward tip of Long Island, consisting of Hither Hills and Montauk Point, and was one of the original investors in the Brooklyn Bridge. Grandpa Hoe was a founder of the Metropolitan Museum of Art and his grandfather was the inventor of the Hoe printing press, which catapulted printing into the twentieth century. My mother's grandmother was a James, and the James family flourished and prospered on both sides of the Atlantic. Arthur Curtis James had a yacht that rivaled Cleopatra's barge. Audrey James was beloved of the Prince of Wales before he met Mrs. Simpson and fell on evil times. And Cousin Venetia James lived in the most fabulous houses in both London and the lovely English countryside, where as a girl I would visit, in fear and trembling of her terrifying temper and equally terrifying benevolences. Her houses were aquiver with cymbidium orchids and celebrities, and every last lamb chop was counted, for if there was anything Cousin Venetia detested it was extravagant waste. She owned a series of regal chow dogs who were as unpredictable and as formidable as their mistress.

My father remains a shadowy, enchanted figure, for I was almost too young to remember him when he died. When I was ten years old my mother remarried. My stepfather, Harold Fowler, was an Irishman. North Ireland. He was a man of great charm and wit, with a universal reputation for bravery. He served in both the British and American air forces in World War One, with the distinction of being the youngest colonel in the American Army. At the end of the war he flew his fighter plane through the Arc de Triomphe, having left his youth and most of his hair behind in the war-torn skies above France and Germany. Most of his life he served his country in Military Intelligence, and while none of his exploits were ever told, an aura of heroism irradiated the man and everything he touched. He twice rode his own horse in the Grand National steeplechase at Aintree, and the fact that he never managed to complete the course in no way detracted from the feat in the eyes of his friends and family. In World War Two he served first in the Canadian Air Force and then in the American. The plane in which he was riding was shot down over North Africa and he pulled the unconscious pilot from the cockpit seconds before the machine blew up, this in spite of having a broken leg himself. The force of the explosion
X threw him and the pilot to the ground, but Harold's body

shielded the pilot, who was not seriously hurt, although Harold was very nearly killed. Between the two world wars, when he was not serving missions for Military Intelligence and riding in the Grand National, he served as deputy chief of police of New York City under Mayor Fiorello La Guardia.

Harold and my mother were very different, but they complemented each other and theirs was a remarkably happy marriage. He died at the age of seventy; my mother never recovered from his death and died a few short years after he did.

With my background and upbringing, it seemed the most natural thing on earth that all the large ranches in that part of Nevada where I came to live belonged, or had belonged, to families of Scotch, English, Irish, and Welsh descent.

I had married a Scotch-Irish rancher called Dick Magee. My mother-in-law was one of the beautiful Dean girls whose father, Joe Dean, had founded the Dean Ranch in Crescent Valley and whose grandfather, Simeon Wenban, owned and operated the Cortez silver mine in Cortez Canyon.

Theirs was the Anglo-American world the ethnographers love to define as the moving force in the settling of the Far West. Theirs were the names and traditions. And where are they now? Gone like the snows of yesteryear. Dead or departed. Of the old names and families, only a few are left.

Sometimes, I wonder what happened to all the tall sons and lovely daughters. Where did they go? The lines died out. The younger generations moved away, never to return. But the stories remain, haunting the empty homesteads and echoing through the lonely canyons. How mad and bad and beautiful they were, those early settlers of the range. They made the myth of the Westerners, and it killed them. They did not breed on. Men and women alike, those giants of another age are gone and the names associated with the ranches today are Italian and German and Basque.

Let me tell you some of the stories of those early Central Nevadans. Of the violence and valor and the tremendous charm that tinged even their most prosaic actions with magic. These stories are not history, meticulously researched and **xi** documented and wrung dry of flesh and blood. These are stories that neighbors and family tell, where fact grows just a little larger than life. This is the stuff of legend.

xii

PART ONE:
Central Nevada Memories

The Never-Never Houses of Nevada

STRANGE THINGS are hidden in the interior of Nevada, and strangest of all are the great country houses built there by a generation of dreamers now gone, as mirages fade at dusk over the dry lakes. Of these houses, once so splendid, rising turreted and towered, separated from each other by miles of sagebrush and silence, magnificent, impractical, and utterly incredible, little remains. The few who saw them have forgotten their existence. And I too might have forgotten if I had not lived in one of them for nearly ten years. Its high ceilings and gracious shadows haunt me yet. Often I think of it, and of the houses like it that briefly flowered in the desert.

The first time I saw the Grass Valley house, I was not as surprised as I would have been had I known Nevada better. I had lived in Europe, where country houses and a certain formality in living are traditional, and the West was new to me. But even on that first visit I found something wonderfully sad and fascinating in the peeling paint, closed doors, and shrouding dust of the old house. To keep it up would have required a staff of scrubbers and polishers, headed by some silently bowing butler. But instead, an Indian matron shuffled casually from kitchen to dining room, and the rest of the house made out as best it could. Nobody spent any time there anyway. Life was centered outdoors, and the floors were littered with boots and saddle blankets, and bridles draped the walls. Under the occupational clutter I glimpsed marble-topped tables and carved rosewood. They glimmered faintly up at me like drowned maidens from the bottom of the sea. **3**

It would be foolish to say I went to live at Grass Valley for the sake of the house. But after I made it my home the house reached out and clutched me. Slowly at first, and then with more and more enthusiasm, I began to notice it, to cherish it, to restore it to some of its former grace.

This was no functional ranch house. It was not functional at all. No concession had been made by its builders to the ferocious mountains and shimmering wastes that surrounded it. It was the bland reincarnation of some rich Victorian vision; of tiny chairs ornately carved, gilt-touched, brocaded; massive bedsteads looming darkly; velvet and plush; lace curtains; even a peeping cupidon laughing up at me from a cluttered corner.

The house had been built in 1870 at a time when lumber had to be hauled by ox team from the Sierra Nevada two hundred miles away, and when furniture was consigned by ship around the Horn and then freighted laboriously inland from California. The builder of the house had made a fortune in silver. The first men who made their money in Nevada mines, bonanza kings of the Comstock and the rest, moved away. Their wives were obsessed with social longings and quickly gratified them in San Francisco, New York, London, Paris, or Rome. Few lingered in Nevada. But by the time Central Nevada mines were established, a new breed of prospector had developed. The men who had explored the wild, free country for years were under its spell. Some of them invested their money in ranches, and to these ranches brought their wives. But the wives, suddenly so wealthy, must have material evidence of this wealth—grand pianos, Oriental rugs, German silver, cut glass, and peacock feathers.

One indomitable woman, whose husband struck it rich, poured every penny he made into a pleasure dome to rival Kubla Khan's. Barely had the house been completed to the last tessellated turret when the lode ran out. Here were the couple, encumbered with a gingerbread palace situated in a wilderness, their money gone. The husband took to his armchair—carved mahogany and black tufted leather. But his wife lived triumphantly in her strange palace. Her children worked

4

the land, hay was harvested, cattle increased and flourished. And when the husband was found dead in his chair she had him carried to a knoll with a fine view of the house that killed him and there, to this day, he lies. The woman lived on and on, a demon of energy driving her, and her children worked and worked. If one of them dared think of leaving the place, he roused the terrible rage of the old woman. And when, finally, she died, she wrote such a will that her children, their children, and their children's children were forced to stay on the home ranch. Even after death she watched over her house, and any descendant she suspected of harboring inclinations to get away, she haunted, slamming doors and rattling chains. In time she lost all discrimination in her haunting, and the house became uninhabitable. Lawyers were called in, the will was ultimately broken, her descendants scattered. The present owner lives in a small cottage at the far end of the ranch and the gingerbread palace is abandoned.

Even when such houses are not haunted, in these days of no servants and busy living few care to live in them. One such I found in Smoky Valley. I had been directed to a particular ranch, and seeing, far out in the center of the valley, a large house, I thought to find the rancher there. The road seemed little traveled, but it was winter, a time when people stay close to home. Scattered snow clouds chased each other high overhead, with still intervals of pale sunlight. The sun was shining when I reached the house and got out of my car. The house was grey, built of adobe brick, and the light of the winter afternoon washed it with gold. It stood on a rise of ground, and all around lay the gray, desolate alkali flats. It took only a glance to tell me no one lived there. Windows gaped, doors fell from hinges. But the pale sunlight wove a web of sleeping enchantment over the ruin. I peered inside at long, low-ceilinged rooms. Outside were the remains of a lovely garden. Regretfully I left, and found in time the rancher's wife in a pre-fab cottage at the edge of the highway. "I've been to the old house," I said. "It is so lovely." And in all innocence, I asked, "Why don't you live there?" "Live there!" she howled. "The place is a woman killer!"

5

It was not dread of housework but the demonetization of silver that caused the forsaking of the pillared house in Cortez Canyon. Built throughout of hardwood, it stood for years under the shadow of Tenabo Mountain, facing on the giant silver ledge from which its owner had made his fortune. At one time the canyon teemed with life; a camp of Chinese mine laborers spread below the house, forges rang, ore wagons pulled by twenty-horse teams strained up the winding road, tailings washed from the mill at the base of the mine, and the muffled report of dynamite vied with shrilling kyatz birds as the work of tunneling the mountain went on. By the time I knew it the mine was closed, the mill stood idle, and the gracious white house was empty, open to the winds.

Of all the formal, foolish houses of an earlier age, only the Grass Valley house flourished and grew younger and handsomer with the passing years. Originally it had not been large, but a second, new house was tacked on to it in the early nineteen hundreds. This second house became the kitchen and dining room, while upstairs its attic was made over into a sort of apartment where I hid those belongings of mine I felt did violence to the Victorian spirit of the house. Some bathrooms had been scattered through it, and I introduced a few closets. Much of the furniture had been my husband's great-grandfather's, and in the living room I placed a grand piano that had supposedly belonged to Mark Twain's brother.

None of the modern nonsense about a house fitting into the landscape troubled the Grass Valley house. It stood on an eminence in the center of the valley and challenged the mountains with its high red rooftops. It could be seen for miles in every direction. Built of California redwood shiplap painted white, deep porches shaded it on every side. Its walls were double and filled with sawdust on the insulating principle of old icehouses. When storm winds raged up the open valley the house met them head on, moaning and shuddering at each fresh impact of the gale. In winter when the temperature dropped below zero the rafter beams cracked loudly as they contracted against the bitter cold. But inside it was always comfortable. A huge fireplace heated the immense living

6

room, and vents carried its heat through the rest of the house. In summer, with blinds drawn and windows shut, on the hottest day the house stayed cool. It was a house of atmospheres, each room subtly different from the others, but to me it was always a friendly house, responding to my love with a love of its own. We were very different, the house and I. And yet we understood each other, and while I did many things for the house it in turn did many things for me. The treasures hidden away in its dark corners it would produce like magic gifts: a silver spoon, a purple bottle, a yellowed paper, and once, a rare first edition of Mark Twain's *Gilded Age*. And then one day the house caught fire.

Like a tinsel toy it went in a puff—the old lumber, the sawdust between the walls, the pane of glass on which the first owner had scratched his name—in an hour it was ash. Sometimes I look at the site where it used to stand and imagine I see it still, its small-paned windows gleaming, shadows deep under its long porches, its carved, straight-rising columns, and all around it a whir and shimmer of jewel-bright hummingbirds. Since the house burned the hummingbirds come no more to the valley.

A Sprig of Sage for Black Pete

"WHO IS THAT MAN who rides alone?" I asked John Callaghan.

He glanced in the direction I was looking.

It was a cold day in late November, and some of us were riding after cattle. With hats tugged low, coat collars turned over our ears, we were muffled like haystacks against the icicle cold. But the solitary horseman sat straight and spare on his lean roan horse, impervious alike to weather or companionship. His face was stern and somber, and the clothes he wore were somber too. Levi's and Levi jumper, heavy leather chaps stained almost black with use, black boots well worn, and a

7

dark felt hat pulled over one eye. The only touch of color about his person was, tied tight around his throat, a scrap of purple silk, as gay and incongruous on that bleak winter day as a snatch of song.

"Him?" said John Callaghan. "Don't you know him?" And when I shook my head, "That's Pete," he told me. "Black Pete."

Not until after his death did I ever hear his full name, Peter Etcheverry. As Black Pete he was known and as Black Pete he will be remembered.

Black Pete was French Basque. He came to America as a very young man in 1903. With the exception of a short time spent in Fresno, California, his entire life was lived on the high mountains and in the wind-swept valleys of Central Nevada.

The first place Black Pete went to work when he arrived in Nevada from France was the Grass Valley Ranch. At that time George Wingfield owned Grass Valley and the ranch was managed by Ed Perez. Those were wild, lawless days on the open range. Sheepman fought sheepman and the cattlemen fought the sheep. The Grass Valley sheep ranged the length and breadth of Central Nevada, and with them went Black Pete, a shepherd's crook in one hand and a rifle in the other.

After Wingfield sold out in 1915 Pete went to work for John Laborde. Speaking of those times, John Laborde said, "Pete was a fine man."

But those very qualities that made Black Pete such a fine man, also made him hard to work with. Fiery, fearless, and ferociously loyal, his fierce rages were famous. He was a solitary man, a man who needed the vast sweep of the wild Nevada range, a man who soon felt confined and restless in towns, a man who did his best work alone.

When Big John Ansolabehere put Black Pete to herding sheep, he felt grave doubts as to whether he or anyone else would be able to get along with Pete. It is a tribute to both men that not only did Black Pete spend the rest of his life working for Big John, tending first his sheep and then his cattle as faithfully and conscientiously as though they were his

8

own and riding range in fair weather and foul, but that over and above duty theirs was a deep and lasting friendship.

Sometimes I would ask Black Pete about the Old Country and whether he ever felt a desire to return to France. "Never!" he would cry. "There is nothing for me there. All my life has been in Nevada. Nevada is my country, my home!" And he would scowl at the surrounding mountains like an old eagle surveying his domain.

There lay the real trouble. An old eagle, not a young eagle. Straight though Pete sat his horse, hard though he drove himself, he was growing old. And he took a sort of stubborn pride, not so much in his own age as in the extreme longevity of his immediate family. He used to tell me of parents and uncles and aunts and grandparents, and it seemed to me each and every one of them lived triumphantly past the hundred mark. But old age was not for Pete. He neither desired nor provided for it. All his life he earned good wages, and as he earned he spent.

In spite of friendships, in spite of his devotion to the Ansolabeheres, I always think of Black Pete as I first saw him, riding apart, riding through life alone. The man who rides alone carries a heavy burden, a burden that must with advancing years become intolerable. And so it proved for Pete.

Because of the violent and tragic nature of Pete's death, those who were his friends have naturally asked themselves how they failed him. However life itself may have failed Black Pete, there was nothing lacking in the abiding affection his friends the Ansolabeheres gave him. Their home was his home.

Those of us who knew him grieve that he is gone, that we shall never again hear his melodious whistle reverberating against the canyon walls, or share in his quick laughter and wry jokes. For Pete had a quality of humor hidden beneath his brusque manner that was as charming as it was unexpected.

Gathered to bid their old friend a last farewell were men who had been young when Pete was young, stern-faced men who had worked with him a lifetime. Although there were flowers on the casket, an outsider attending the funeral might

9

have wondered why those of us who came from far away, from remote ranches over the abominable roads, from Reno and Battle Mountain and elsewhere, such an outsider might have wondered why we brought with us so few flowers to lay on Black Pete's grave.

Indeed, somebody did remark on the lack of flowers, to which retorted one of those who knew Pete best:

"No flowers for Black Pete. We bury him the way he lived, with a bottle of whiskey and a sprig of sage!"

Sarvice Berries

YESTERDAY WE RODE up Steiner Canyon hunting for cows. It was a clear day, after nearly a week of heavy thunderstorms, and the leaves of the cottonwoods trembled with greenness, the air was pungent and aromatic. Far up the canyon we passed through a glade carpeted with wild mint. Crushed under the feet of our horses the mint-smell rose around us, wonderfully fresh and fragrant.

With the sleek cattle bunched ahead, we started for home. In the golden evening light I noticed a small, solitary tree laden with berries and asked what kind they were. "Sarvice berries," I was told.

Sarvice berries—magic word. Although I had heard of them and even seen trees, I had never before seen one bearing fruit. So many of the mountain men ate sarvice berries and thought to mention it in the meager records they left of their lives: Jedediah Smith, the great explorer; Joe Walker, the first to kill Indians along the Humboldt; Peter Skeene Ogden, the gentle English fur trader; and reckless Bartleson. All of them. And those gay, laughing figures who fill the early pages of the *Reese River Reveille,* they too feasted on sarvice berries.

10 I plucked one of the fruits from the little tree. It was bluish purple, tasting something like a tiny plum, something like a blueberry, and evoking with its flavor all those departed figures of Nevada history who once ate sarvice berries.

The White Doe

ALTHOUGH COPIES of the *Sazerac Lying Club* are so scarce that there is hardly a volume left in Austin of Fred Hart's famous book, every old-time resident has heard of the immortal "Club."

Fear that I might be considered a prevaricator has restrained me from telling of an unusual experience which befell one summer. It was only after reading some words in an old history of Nevada that I decided to write about it. The history said: "The Sazerac Lying Club was one of the most flourishing institutions ever in Austin, leaving an influence still felt in the community, and an example fondly emulated by many now alive."

To quote directly from the pages of the *Sazerac Lying Club* itself, it says of its members: "We do not lie for greed or gain. While we permit a range of thought extending far away into the most distant depths of the realm of the impossible and the improbable, we do not stoop to the lie of deceit."

It is into those realms, far away and distant, that my story goes.

There are many Indian legends told of Mount Callaghan, and of Skull Creek which has its source in snowbanks high on the slopes of the old mountain. I never ride up its canyons without feeling that something strange and beautiful is waiting for me around the next turn.

There is no hostility in the wild scenery of Mount Callaghan. Riding there, alone, I never feel that inexplicable uneasiness and alarm which I have known in parts of the Simpson 11

Park range. The hills of Shagnasty crouch like great cats waiting to spring, Bates Mountain is a lonely place, and the reaches of Steiner Canyon are dark and haunted.

The cattle do not share my preference for the Toiyabe over the Simpson Park range; I must ride both sides of the valley equally. However, on the August day of which I write I was riding up Skull Creek.

Once past the big spring I saw many sage hen. They were strutting their pompous, tip-toe walk. At my approach they would squat behind a bush and, with slender necks ridiculously extended, watch me, their eyes alert. Then, with a whir of wings, they would fly away. Deer bounded up the sidehills. As they paused at the top for a long look at me, the antlers of the bucks rose like candelabra against the blue curtain of the sky.

The forks of Skull Creek network the face of the mountain, draining at different levels into the main fork. I was riding down a lesser fork, and had reached its juncture with the main fork, which I planned to ascend, when I noticed a white object move in some willows on the face of the hill opposite me. At first I thought it was a white yearling calf, or possibly a sheep strayed from its flock. It was partly obscured by the willows. As it made no further movement, I could not see it clearly with the naked eye. From my saddle I took a pair of field glasses and focused them on the white animal. Just as I had it squarely in range, it walked slowly out of the protection of the trees. It stood motionless, its head turned toward me so that we were face to face. And I realized that I was looking at a white doe.

She was not alarmed by the sight of me, nor were the other five does that grazed near her. After a perfunctory glance at me, they continued to feed, and I was able to study the white deer. She was not an albino, for her eyes were brown. The tips of her ears and the extremities of her legs and short tail were shaded gray, while down the center of her back ran a pale gray line, like the black line down the back of a buckskin horse. Except for these gray markings she was pure white.

All the way home, and for many days thereafter, my mem-

12

ory was filled with the sight of the white deer, mingling with remembered stories of fable and enchantment.

How to Bake Bread with a "Green Jacket, Red Cap, and White Owl's Feather"

IF YOU WANT TO BAKE your own bread, there's no use being modern about it. A good bread-baker goes back, mentally, a long way, back to the days of goblins and elves and water sprites, back to those odd unpredictable ages when Little Men roamed abroad. The Little Men have been driven into hiding. Shy, and perhaps a shade vindictive, they lurk in a few forgotten places. And one of the places where they lurk is in bread —homemade bread. If you don't believe me, let me tell you a story.

I was making bread. Beneath my hands the dough was resilient. Through the east window streamed an early morning sun. It had been cold that night, but it was warming up fast. A bottomless blue sky towered above snow-topped mountains, and the sun shining on the lone willow touched its bare twigs with gold.

The board I work my dough on fits into a slight depression in the drainboard of the kitchen sink. The sink was full of hot, soapy water into which I planned shortly to pop the mixing bowl and other utensils I had used. I was very efficient at that early hour, efficient and I must admit more than a little pleased with myself. At last, after years of intermittent effort, I had mastered the knack of making good bread. I did not merely *hope,* I *knew* the bread I was kneading would turn into large lovely loaves.

It is curious that no cookbook, however well written, can teach a person who has never made bread how to do it. Follow directions as closely as you can: The bread will fail to rise, or it will rise at the top and lie in sodden layers on the bottom; **13** it will be as full of holes as Swiss cheese; it will be as dry and grainy as the sands of Sahara. In turn my earlier attempts had passed through all these incarnations. But eventually I had triumphed. My bread was edible. More, it was delicious.

And as I kneaded the dough, feeling the first bubbles form and burst as I pushed and gently pressed, it came to me I should share with others this art, so hard come by, of making bread successfully. I would write an article . . .

No sooner thought, the warm smug glow of creation barely born, than I felt the dough—the dough I *knew* would make such lovely bread—leap in my hands. It rose, the fat, pale moon-blob rose through the air, then sank beneath the surface of the soapy scalding dishwater.

Suicide.

I watched it drown, irrevocable as Humpty Dumpty's fall from the wall. Then, as the waters swirled over it, I glimpsed, peering at me through the suds, the wickedly grinning face of a Little Man. I had forgotten the Little Men!

Little Men wait in the yeast like actors in the wings; they wait their cue to bound out of the yeast packet into the tempestuous world of the mixing bowl. But active though they are, you must remember they are old—terribly, terribly old. Age makes them delicate and crochety, like fierce old men who tire quickly and feel the cold.

So the first thing to do with them is to get them warm. Prepare a teacup to receive them. Put in it a quarter of a cup of tepid water and a teaspoon and a half of sugar. They do like sugar. Now crumble two cakes of fresh yeast into the teacup; let it sit about five minutes—then stir it thoroughly. I always stir my yeast with a small, thin silver spoon. It is a frail old spoon and I don't use it for anything else. The Little Men are fond of it and I keep it just for them.

Set the teacup in a warm, comfortable place. If conditions are right, surroundings agreeable, and the stars propitious, in about fifteen minutes the Little Men will be moving about. The cup will be full to the brim with a fine froth of bubbles. If it is not, wait until it is. And if it never starts to seethe and foam, do something else with the batter you've been mixing, for whatever else it may make, it won't make bread.

14

For three loaves of bread you will need (besides the yeast):
    a large mixing bowl,
    a wooden spoon,
    a saucepan,
    salt, sugar, butter or margarine,
        milk, and potato water,
    about nine cups of flour.
Put three tablespoons of butter, three tablespoons of sugar, and one tablespoon of salt in the mixing bowl. Scald one and a half cups of milk in the saucepan and pour it on top of the ingredients in the bowl. Stir with the wooden spoon until the butter is melted and the sugar and salt are dissolved. If the potato water has been stored in the refrigerator, put a cup and a half of it into the saucepan and warm it just enough to take the chill off. If it is already at room temperature, add it to the mixture without heating. Then add four cups of the flour, stirring vigorously, a cup at a time.

When the batter is well-blended and smooth, go take a look at the Little Men in the teacup of yeast. Are they vigorous? Are they prancing around and ready to jump out of the cup? If they are, you may proceed with confidence. Pour them into the batter and stir. Stir and stir and stir until your arm gives out. Then try stirring with the other arm, in all about ten minutes. The circular motion exhilarates the Little Men like a ride on a merry-go-round.

When you are sure they must be dizzy, set the mixing bowl in a warm, secluded spot and give them a chance to get their breath. And give yourself a chance to do the same. In about ten minutes or so you should all be ready for the next step.

Gradually stir in enough of the remaining flour (about four cups) to make a thick, rather stiff dough. As you mix in the flour, keep scraping the side of your bowl—it will be almost clean by the time the dough is stiff. Don't try to hurry. The Little Men are old and they detest being rushed.

Flour a board with some of the cup of flour you have left. Turn the dough out on it and start to knead.

If you have ever watched someone who knows how to knead, you will be familiar with the technique. If not, this is **15** what you do: Fold the dough toward you with a rolling motion with the fingers of both hands, then push the dough away with the heels of your hands. Turn dough one quarter way around on the board and repeat the folding and pushing. Do this over and over. Be sure the board is in a place where it will not skid. At first the dough will be sticky and lumpy. Sprinkle a little of the extra flour on it to keep it from fastening to your fingers like glue. As you work it, the stickiness will disappear. Add flour only until the dough no longer sticks to your hands or the board. When enough has been added, the dough will be smooth and the glueyness will have gone. And the lumps will go, too. Don't look at the clock while you knead. If you have a window with a pleasant view, look out the window. But keep kneading. And don't work at it. Just lean on your hands and let the heels of them sink in the dough, then lightly pluck the dough back with your fingertips. Do not be rough, do not hurry, and do not forget the Little Men. Soon you will feel them under your hands. Bubbles will form in the dough and queer sighings will come out of it. As more and larger bubbles form, they will break with a tiny smacking sound. When this happens, you know the dough has been worked long enough.

Place it in a large, greased mixing bowl. And then turn the dough over so that what was on the bottom is on top. This will coat the dough with shortening and prevent a crust from forming. Dampen a clean dish towel, wring it out, and lay it over the bowl. Set it in a warm, quiet spot. Remember the age and delicate health of the Little Men. No drafts, no disturbances, no cold. Go away and leave matters to them. If you come back in about an hour, the dough should be peeking at you over the top of the bowl.

At this point keep a poker face. It is too early for a show of confidence. Lots of things can still go wrong. Grimly lift off the cloth and punch the dough right in its middle. It will give a heartbreaking sigh and collapse. Punch it some more and turn it over. Cover it and leave.

More quickly than the first time the dough will rise, filling the bowl and puffing up the cloth. In about 45 minutes, when it has risen as high as or higher than it did the first time, give it a poke to deflate it and flop it out of the bowl onto the board. Knead it into a ball and then cut it into three parts. Make three balls and set them side by side on the board for about ten minutes. Grease three bread pans, 9 x 5 x 3. Aluminum pans are good, although I prefer glass ones because I can see what is going on inside.

Lightly shape each ball into a rectangle, 10 x 9. Using both hands, fold the two shorter edges to the middle. Pinch the edges together to seal and put each loaf in a pan, making sure the pinched side is down. Cover the pans with a damp towel and place them side by side in their quiet corner. Be sure it is not too warm, for excessive heat will make the loaves rise too much.

About an hour later, when the dough has risen in the pans, put the pans in a hot oven (400°). About 30 minutes later look in the oven. Do not snatch the loaves out and start eating them. Instead tap them lightly with your fingers. If they have a hollow sound, brush their little faces with melted butter or margarine and let them bake another 10 minutes.

Turn the loaves out of the pans the minute you take them out of the oven. Wrap them in a clean, dry dish towel and set them on a cake rack to cool. The towel will keep the crust tender and enable the Little Men, their work done, to creep away unseen, like actors sheltered by the final curtain.

The longer you can bear to wait, the easier it will be to slice your bread. But the sooner you eat it, the better it will taste. The perfect temperature is cool enough not to burn your fingers but hot enough to melt the butter or margarine.

Unless you are a very large gathering, you will not eat all the bread while it is hot. When what is left has cooled, wrap it in waxed paper and store it in the breadbox. The potato water you used to make it will help keep it moist and fresh for several days. Then it will be time to call up the Little Men and bake again.

This recipe is for basic bread. Once it is mastered, the most recherché yeast recipes that cookbooks can devise will be **17**

yours for the baking. But you must remember always to
leaven the loaf with just one touch of necromancy.

Why I Stopped Riding Sidesaddle

18 WHEN I CAME to live on a cattle ranch in the emptiest part of
Central Nevada, I brought my sidesaddle with me. And what

is more, I rode on it. Plodding through dust behind cows, scrambling up and down mountain peaks, breaking colts— over the hoots and jeers of friends, family, and neighbors— I rode sidesaddle.

"Why not use a stock saddle like other people do?" they used to ask.

"Wild horses couldn't change the way I ride!" I would retort.

But wild horses did.

North of our ranch, in the rough, wooded hills west of Mount Tenabo, range herds of mustangs. Little, tough, intelligent horses, they have outsmarted and outrun mustang hunters for years. Not until my husband Dick Magee started hunting them with his plane—a 140 Cessna—were these mustangs caught in any quantity. Most of the horses Dick caught were sold, although we kept a few of the best looking for seed stock, branding and turning them back out on the open range. And of course some of the colts fell to me.

The colt I liked best was a pumpkin-colored buckskin with four white-stockinged legs and a blaze face. I called him Toomi. Toomi was pleasant to handle. He never got excited. He never kicked or fought or tried to buck. But he was terribly hard to ride—that is, to ride with a sidesaddle. His back was round and boneless as a sofa pillow, and however tight I cinched my saddle on, it would sway sickeningly from left to right and finally settle under Toomi's fat tummy.

I borrowed an old stock saddle, set it on Toomi, and tried a few cautious rides. The saddle stayed securely in place: I was the one who wobbled. It still makes me ache to remember the first long ride I made on Toomi astride. Muscles unused since my early days at Foxcroft School creaked and moaned like old oak timbers. If Toomi had not had a quite remarkable personality, I would have given up riding him then and there. But he was more companion than horse, and for the sake of being with him, I endured the stock saddle.

I soon found getting off and on was easier (and safer) riding astride; the mountains seemed less precipitous, my horses more docile. Best of all, I was able to join in the ranch work **19** of roping and branding calves. With no horn on which to take a dally, this had been impossible for me to do before.

Dust began to settle on my sidesaddle.

And now, if anybody needs a sidesaddle, I have one hanging idle from the rafters in the granary. Wild horses got me off it, but it would take more than a wild horse—even one as charming as Toomi—to get me back on it again.

20

PART TWO:
Archaeology on Horseback

The Stones of the Blue Sky Magic

TURQUOISE IS A PRODIGAL TREASURE. I have seen uncut
stones heaped ankle- deep in a dusty yard, and along the bare,
brassy shores of the Persian Gulf, children gather it like pebbles. In Nevada an old man telling of a strike said, "Turquoise! We scooped it into wheelbarrows, every shovelful
worth a hundred dollars." And the old man's eyes snapped
with glee at the recollection, blue eyes strong and bright as
bits of turquoise.

Most American turquoise comes from Nevada, and the
finest grade is found in the high, lonely reaches of the Central
Nevada ranges. The loneliest place I know lies north of Grass
Valley, and here on the desolate rim of a dry lake, backed by
a waterless waste of broken hills, hot springs bubbling like a
witches' caldron nearby, is a mine the experts agree has produced the most beautiful turquoise ever seen in this country.
That mine, the property of Jimmy Allen, is now exhausted and
stands abandoned. But all around us, in the high Toiyabes, in
the Simpson Park Range, near Cortez, and in the bald, black
hills beyond Battle Mountain, turquoise is being mined.

A piece of unpolished turquoise was given me when I first
came to Grass Valley, and I have it still, the turquoise blue
breaking through rough, grey matrix like fragments of sky
between clouds. I would have had it mounted if there had
been anyone here to do the work, but stones are almost always
sent south to the Indians of New Mexico and to the tribes
along the Mexican border in Arizona.

23

There are ways and ways of mounting turquoise. It can be bulged from its setting like gumdrops in cake icing, or sunk flat and smooth in beaten silver. It is the Zuñis who do the delicate work, inlaying the stones, matching and mating and binding them together in hand-wrought metal. I have a concha Zuñi belt made of hundreds of teardrop stones arranged in sun-rays and knobbed with silver, so exquisite it might have been the work of a native Cellini.

Years ago a turquoise buyer came through the ranch, a sharp, gypsy-like man driving a derelict car loaded down with Navajo blankets. He tried to trade us out of a horse, offering to pay his part with multi-colored rugs and Indian jewelry. And the horse that took his fancy was an albino, a queer pale-eyed animal with pink skin and a mane and tail like bridal ribbon. Perhaps he meant to hang its neck with turquoise like an Arab's steed, for the Arabs believe turquoise is a charm to ward off the evil eye. All through the Arab world horses, camels, and long-eared donkeys wear necklaces of blue beads.

The name, turquoise, is French. It means simply Turkish and comes to us from the time of the Crusades, when Christian battled Infidel, when Europeans first saw the blue stones from Persia. Turquoise was then and has remained a stone for the dark-skinned races, a pure, passionate stone inextricably mingled with the mythology of strange, exotic peoples, of Incas, Zuñis, Navajos, Shoshones, of Persians and the nomadic tribes of Islam.

When I was a girl studying in London, on my way to King's College I used to pass a dingy curio shop. Among moth-eaten remnants of other times stuffed helter-skelter in its narrow window was a pair of earrings; from slender gold wires hung two tiny turquoises. In that drab window, under drenching winter skies, those two little stones shone like a promise of happiness, of sunlight and laughter and faraway places. Passing the window I would pause, flatten my nose against the pane, then with a sigh walk on. The earrings were unattainable. It was not the trifling price that put them beyond reach but the fact that they were made for pierced ears, for shell-fluted Moorish ears, harem ears, for any ears but my round

24

American ears with their smooth, unscarred lobes.

One day as I was going by the curio shop I turned on impulse and pushed open the door. A bell clanged and from the stuffy recesses of a back room waddled a slovenly fat woman along whose upper lip flourished a black moustache. At my request she plucked the earrings from the window, blew the dust from them with a great poof from her whiskered mouth, and slapped them down on the counter under my nose. I hardly glanced at them. What need? I had already looked so long. I paid the whiskered woman the few shillings she demanded and fled with the earrings held tight in my hand.

But the imagined joys of possession failed to materialize. Although the earrings were mine, I could not wear them. They would languish forever, as useless in my bureau drawer as they had been in the curio shop window, unless I had my ears pierced. Why not? Dimly I remembered a horrid episode in *Eight Cousins* with a cork, a needle, and a lot of blood. I even found cork and needle and waved them around with a synthetic air of purpose. Friends shudderingly refused to help. My last resort was to go to a doctor to have the job done. When they left me in England my family had given me the name of a Harley Street practitioner, and it was to this gentleman's establishment I betook myself. Waiting in his austerely sombre dining room, thumbing through ancient periodicals while a blend of boiled cabbage and ether crinkled my nose, I felt my courage seep like soup from a cracked bowl. When finally confronted by the great man I was beyond resistance as he solemnly took my pulse. Gravely he inquired into my trouble.

"It's my ears."

In tones deep and rich as molasses, "Do they pain you much?" he asked.

"Oh, not at all. My ears feel fine. It's just—it's just—" my voice trailed away. Then in a burst I blurted, "I want them pierced!"

25

Those earrings were Persian turquoise, the stones a flat, hard blue like nothing seen in this country. Turquoise varies enormously not only in different countries but in different mines, and a turquoise expert can identify which mine a stone comes from as unfailingly as a wine taster can identify vintages. One of the loveliest of all turquoises is spiderweb, mosaicked with fine lines like golden cobwebs across a blue moon.

I had a broken ring—a cracked garnet in a silver and gold setting. The setting was good, and I thought it would be fun to replace the garnet with turquoise. Many turquoise mines now active in Nevada are owned or leased by the Edgar brothers. Some of their mines produce spiderweb turquoise. As well as mining, the Edgar family also operates a small chain of stores along Highway 80 where turquoise jewelry is sold. One of these stores is in the lobby of Battle Mountain's hotel. Driving by one day, I stopped in Battle Mountain and went to the hotel. The Edgars' jewelry counter was locked and there was no sign of Mrs. Edgar. A desk clerk told me she had gone to Salt Lake and would not be back for several days.

"Is her husband in town?" I wanted to know.

The clerk shook his head dubiously. "You could never find his place."

"Battle Mountain isn't that big!" I cried. "Why can't I find him? Where does he live?"

Reluctantly the clerk gave me directions, adding cryptically, "If you see a concrete mixer running, you'll know Edgar's home."

The concrete mixer was running. I heard it before I reached the place. And as I drove into the yard, the mixer upended and spewed forth a torrent of turquoise. Long wooden troughs were heaped with turquoise. Turquoise spilled in blue profusion from end to end of the dusty yard, and when I stepped from my car I stumbled through turquoise like a wader in a shallow sea. Overhead the great cloudless desert sky lifted depth on depth of dazzling blue, and underfoot was reflected as in a mirror the same fabulous blueness.

26

Some tourists, intrigued by my conversation with the desk clerk, had followed me from the hotel, and I heard them ask politely if it was permissible to touch the wealth of pebbles rioting around our feet. I had not thought to ask permission. Down on my knees, I had already buried my arms to the elbows in turquoise.

The tourists had a hundred questions, and patiently Edgar answered them all, explaining that these stones were turquoise nuggets, and that he ran the ore through a concrete mixer to separate the nuggets from the country rock that encased them. "Further south," he said, "turquoise comes in another kind of formation, in layers, what we call cap rock."

In cap rock was found the kind of turquoise our local Shoshone Indians used to work, heating the ledges with burning mahogany sticks and then dripping cold water on them to make the stone chip. And I thought of a conversation I had one day in Austin with Charlie Schmitlien. "Did the Indians around Austin wear turquoise in the old days?" I had asked.

"Did they!" Charlie's square face drew long in amazement at my ignorance. "Didn't you ever hear of Nicodemus?"

I shook my head, baffled. Nicodemus! The Bible? A Negro spiritual? Some old plantation slave? But I guessed Charlie's Nicodemus was Nevadan. "Never heard of him," I ventured.

"Her," Charlie corrected. "Nicodemus was a squaw. The oldest squaw you ever saw. She was old when Frémont and his men explored Monitor Valley. She died when I was only a kid, but I used to talk to her, ask her questions. She had a terrible temper and questions made her mad, but sometimes she'd tell me stories about the days before the white men came. She wore strings of turquoise beads. But it wasn't her beads I remember most: it was her nails. Each nail was over two inches long. If you brought her food and a knife and fork to eat it with, she'd hurl the knife and fork away and tear the food apart with her fingers. Her nails stuck out like talons, and she was like an old, fierce, taloned eagle all festooned with turquoise beads."

Thinking about Charlie and Nicodemus, I knelt in the Battle Mountain yard pouring turquoise nuggets between my **27** fingers,while Edgar went on explaining to the tourists: "Here we grade the turquoise, cut and polish it. Then the stones are sent to the Navajo and Zuñi reservations to be hand set in silver. When he was in America some years back the Shah of Persia sent word he would like me and one of my brothers to come to Iran to show his turquoise workers our methods of cutting and polishing. "Maybe someday we'll go."

When the tourists finally left, gorged with information, he turned inquiringly to me. I held out my empty ring setting. "Can you cut me a stone to fit?"

"Sure," he said. "What kind do you want?"

"Spider, a spiderweb turquoise. I don't see anything here quite the color, but you know—blue."

"Yes," he said. "I know. I know the kind. Are you in a hurry?"

"No hurry. When you find the stone I want, set it in the ring and send it to me. Shall I pay you something down?"

"No." Edgar thrust the ring setting deep in a frayed pocket. "Pay me when you get the ring." And he went back to his churning mixer, water and stones sloshing wildly together with a grumbling, rumbling, rattling noise. I went home.

Later, much later, the ring came, spiderweb turquoise—and blue. Wearing it I remember Nicodemus, the Shahinshah, a whiskered woman in a London curio shop . . .

I wear my turquoise jewelry when I ride, when I work around the ranch, on rare trips to Austin or Elko. But I never wear it with any other jewelry. Turquoise can only be worn with turquoise, and Mexican turquoise clashes with Nevada turquoise, spiderweb does not match the pure blue stones, nugget turquoise is ill-mated with the kind of turquoise found in cap rock. It becomes a hobby, intriguing as stamp collecting, to find a bracelet that will go with a belt, a necklace that fits in, a ring, earrings. And then comes the awful temptation to wear everything at once, like old Nicodemus looped with beads. This must be resisted, for even a little turquoise is suspect in a country where it is almost never worn except by Indians and the arts-and-crafts set. In the rest of the world it enjoys a wider range of wearers, perhaps the widest range

any stone could have, from camels and donkeys to queens and empresses. Among the jeweled Easter eggs of the Russian royal family were turquoise eggs. And I have seen a necklace of pale Persian stones set in gold with diamond pendants that once belonged to Marie Antoinette.

But no one was wearing the loveliest turquoise I ever saw. Riding alone after cattle in the Toiyabe Mountains, I had stopped my winded horse on the very summit of a high, barren peak. I looked out over a tumbled wilderness of empty valleys and soaring hills, all shimmering in the high, thin, desert air. Then looking down I saw thick around my horse's **29** feet chips and fragments of turquoise—a whole mountain top strewn with magic.

A Flake of Flint, A Sherd of Earthenware

THERE IS A WORLD beyond the world we know. A shadow world, where men move silently on naked feet. A world of flickering fires and long nights. A world of snarling predators with gleaming fangs. A world of hunger, cold, and nameless fears. A simple world, whose deep simplicity mystifies the inhabitants of more complex civilizations as a still pool lost in a deep canyon mystifies the observer with its wavering, inverted reflections of overhanging branches.

The greenery reflected in this deep pool is not more evanescent, more intriguing, more beautiful than is the world of prehistory, illumined for a fleeting instant by a pottery sherd or a transluscent fragment of flaked flint.

Archaeology is the study of prehistory through artifacts, those man-made tools and weapons, religious relics, secular ornaments, household goods and garments, those structural remains and monuments which have survived out of the dawn days into our contemporary era.

The science of archaeology has grown increasingly complex as it seeks to rend the clouds of ignorance and reveal the origins of mankind. Related disciplines have been called in, to aid in dating and defining. Methods have been perfected, and discoveries have been made which were undreamed of only a few years ago.

At the 1963 Tule Springs Dig in Southern Nevada, heavy earthmoving equipment was used to trench the valley to depths of many feet, revealing the stratigraphic lines of deposited sediment as clearly as though they had been drawn on a map. Geologists, engineers, dendrochronologists, paleontologists, pollenologists, and others contributed to make the Tule Springs project one of the most ambitious scientifi-

30

cally conducted archaeological studies ever attempted. Tons of earth were moved. Hundreds of thousands of dollars were spent. And the intellectual resources of eminent scientists from all over the world were called upon to unravel the riddle of this site which is considered by some to be the oldest Paleolithic site on the North American continent.

In the face of such professional undertakings, the amateur archaeologist may well question what possible role remains for him in this prohibitively expensive, highly specialized, fiercely competitive field. Assuming the interest of the amateur to be not purely acquisitive but genuinely archaeological, the amateur today plays just as vital a role of discovery as the most highly organized expedition can do. Emphasis must be upon the word *discovery*. Archaeology is too exacting a science for any group of amateurs to hope to develop a site with the expertise demanded by current professional standards.

But cumbersome equipment, batteries of resource personnel, and the thousands of dollars needed for accurate site development are superfluous in the sensitive area of discovery. In discovery of prehistoric sites, the best tools are the least. An observant eye, a contemplative mind, and an eager step remain indispensable for uncovering the all but obliterated traces of prehistory.

As an amateur archaeologist, I share a common interest with other amateurs, whether working individually or in groups. And a brief account of some of my experiences in this field may prove helpful to those with a like avocation.

Two anecdotes will serve to illustrate how much may be accomplished in a given area by an amateur working without specialized equipment, and without collaborators. Above all, it will illustrate how archaeological work can be done without causing destruction to prehistoric evidence which may later serve for more professional research.

These two anecdotes will tell about my first archaeological find at Grass Valley, and one of my most recent. The first tells about a flake of flint, the other about a sherd of earthenware.

Before I came to live in Nevada, my life had been spent either on the eastern seaboard of the Atlantic, in Western

Europe, or traveling in North Africa and parts of Asia. It was quite a contrast from these places to living on a cattle ranch in Central Nevada.

I think the most difficult adjustment I had to make was accustoming myself to the newness of my surroundings. Fresh from the temples of Angkor Wat, the tombs of the Valley of the Kings, the rain-drenched gardens of Versailles, from all such monuments to olden times, I had come to live in a world where history seemed never to go back further than human memory, and where people acted as though a hundred years was an eternity.

The transition tested my powers of adaptability to their limit. I sought salvation in local history and literature. I tried to familiarize myself with the story of the Fur Trade. I studied westerly migration. I researched the early settlements of the surrounding country. I read Angel and Mighels and Sam Davis. I read Mark Twain. I read Bret Harte. I even read his cousin, Fred Hart.

And then one day, driving a bunch of cows and calves up the horse pasture toward the ranch, I stopped my horse in a clump of buck brush to give the slow-moving cattle time to rest. Idly, I glanced at the ground and saw, lying at my horse's feet, a small, leaf-shaped point.

It had a basal notch and bifacial, transverse flaking. Its edges were serrated. And it was made of flint in two tones of light grey. It was about an inch and a half long, and about half an inch broad at its widest point. It is a fairly common type of point for the area. But on that day, when I first saw it, I had never seen anything like it before.

I slipped off my horse and picked it up, holding it cradled in the palm of my hand. As I stared at the leaf-shaped projectile point I felt the past stir around me, with all its rustle of unanswered questions. And I lifted my eyes to a valley which suddenly was peopled with unknown shadows.

What hand had shaped that point? Where? When? Why?

There was nothing stirring in the valley except the cattle, my horse, my dog, and I. But the stone tool in my hand was evidence that people had been there before us. Long, long

before.

I dropped the grey point in my pocket, remounted, and slowly followed the cattle up the pasture, wondering as I rode if the flint in my pocket was just an isolated find or if there might be other artifacts in the valley, other traces of a world older than local history's hundred years. Older, perhaps, than a thousand. Perhaps even old as the Pleistocene.

The questions I asked myself that day have not all been answered. But of the people who lived in Grass Valley in pre-Caucasian times I know more than I would have dreamed possible when I found that first projectile point.

I know now where the Grass Valley people lived, what they ate, how they died, where they lie buried, their strange, high monuments. I know now their goings and their comings up and down the valley. I have found where they quarried the red chert and where the flesh-toned quartz. I know the slopes where they gathered grass seed, the forests where they harvested pine nuts. I have followed the deer trails and stumbled on the haunts of the mountain sheep they stalked. I know their sacred springs, and the high cliffs covered with their petroglyph carvings. I can walk through their winter villages, finding my way from house cluster to house cluster as easily as a suburban housewife visiting friends in a nearby street.

This knowledge came to me gradually over the years. It did not reveal itself all at once. And some evidence that was there I failed to interpret, or even to see, because I did not know enough to look for it. For years I remained blind to bedrock mortars and stone men, looking at them without knowing what I was seeing. It was the same with pottery sherds.

If somebody had told me then that there was pottery scattered the length and breadth of Grass Valley, I would have thought he was joking. Even today, when I see pottery I am not always sure what I am seeing. This happened to me one November as I was bringing a bunch of cattle out of Skull Creek. It was a wild day and windy, with snow flurries. The cattle kept bearing away from the creek toward the south, and I pressed on their flank with my two dogs, herding them in the direction in which I wanted them to go.

The ground was covered with sagebrush and small boulders. I rode a grey mare and as she picked her way I glanced **33** down from time to time, although mostly my eyes were on the flighty cattle. In one particularly rough place I noticed a curious pile of thin, dark grey, almost black, shale-like rocks. But I never thought of stopping to examine them until I had gone some distance, when I began to suspect the shale-like rock might have been pottery. I turned my mare and retraced our steps. Before long I came to the pile I had noticed earlier. I jumped off, and had only to lift one piece to know what it was. I sensed the unmistakable curve of a vessel fragment, and felt its smoothed touch under my fingers. It was earthenware.

There was a big piece of dead sagebrush nearby. I snatched it up and jammed it upside down in a live bush to mark the site. Then I scrambled back on my mare and dashed down the canyon after my cattle, which were fast disappearing into the storm.

Two days passed before I could return to Skull Creek.

Miles Burkett, in his delightful book *The Old Stone Age,* has written, "It is the period of delay between perception and reaction which gives rise to an increase of emotional tension."

During those two days before I could get back to look at my pottery find, I had built up enough "emotional tension" to detonate the whole valley. But when I came within sight of the inverted sagebrush pointing like a beacon to the spot where I had seen the sherds, I did not go directly there. For during the two-day interval I had had ample time to reflect on those sherds, and the more I thought about the place where I had seen them, the more puzzled I became by their location.

Perhaps if I describe some of the more typical Grass Valley pottery sites, I can illustrate what made the Skull Creek site unusual. For example, the first pottery find I made at Grass Valley was in 1959, when I picked up four body sherds of coarse grey Shoshone ware. This site was situated at the foot of a low hill, or hillock, entirely covered with the circular remains of house foundations. Some of these foundations were no more than shallow indentations in the surface of the ground, while others were dug into the slope of the hill to a depth of three or four feet. Flaked stone and ground stone artifacts were strewn in profusion over the surface of the site, as were numerous remains of trade goods. There were kitchen middens scattered among the house foundations. Such a location would seem a normal one in which to find sherds, the probable remains of some pot or cooking vessel.

All my subsequent pottery finds were oriented to the banks of the perennial streams which flow into Grass Valley from the surrounding mountain ranges. And the greatest concentrations of pottery sites were in the vicinity of the winter villages in the middle of the upper, or southerly end of Grass Valley.

Skull Creek is the largest of the tributary Grass Valley streams. It pours steeply out of two great gashes in the flanks of Mount Callaghan, known respectively as North Fork and Main Fork of Skull Creek. The forks meet in the Upper Skull Creek field, where the land begins to level out, and from this point the stream flows into the wide alluvial meadows and hay lands of Grass Valley Ranch.

Quite high in Skull Creek, where it first tumbles out of the great mountain, is a large, circular spring, known, not very imaginatively, as the Big Spring. Below it a series of smaller springs form marshy circles which drain into the creek bed. The land surrounding the Big Spring is rich in artifacts. These consist mostly of projectile points, scrapers, choppers, awls and drills. But a few finely worked specimens of ground stone indicate that this area was not only a hunting site, but also an area of seed-gathering activities.

If ever there were winter villages in Upper Skull Creek, I had found no traces of their house foundations. Although there were campsites on the low hills south of the Skull Creek field, these seemed to be of recent occupancy, and transient. Possibly these sites had been used by Indians cutting wood and quarrying stone for the ranch which for over a hundred years had occupied the center of southern Grass Valley.

On the north side of Skull Creek, on the high bench between the Big Spring and some of the smaller springs directly below it, I had found three pottery sites. These sites were small, each one producing no more than a handful of little body sherds, most of them no bigger than my thumbnail. The type of pottery represented at these sites resembled Owens

Valley brown ware. Because these pottery finds were in an area rich in other artifacts, even though no traces of habitation remained, there was nothing really incongruous in their location.

But the sherds I had found when I was bringing the cattle down the canyon were on the south side of Skull Creek, a little over a quarter of a mile away from water, in a flat, wide, rocky waste. There are flakes of worked flint over most of Skull Creek Canyon, but the action of the torrential waters streaming off the mountain when the snow melts and the spring runoff breaks loose, has pulverized the smaller lithic matter into unrecognizable fragments. Only on the ridges and benches can the artifacts survive the destructive power of the spring floods, bearing their grinding burden of sediment and rock.

Yet, in spite of their perilous location, the sherds I had found were lying in a layered pile. What they were doing there was a question that intrigued me almost as much as did the sherds themselves.

I had driven my jeep up the canyon, and stopped it by the creek, opposite the inverted sagebrush which marked the pottery site. Getting out, I began to walk in a wide circle of which the sagebrush marker formed the geometric center. As I walked I stopped often to search the ground and to scan the surrounding terrain for any clue which might explain the presence of the sherds in that particular location. A grave site seemed the most probable explanation, but no rock cairn, no cottonwood poles, no ritual dish and cup indicated a grave. At least not one from the historic period.

When I finally zeroed in on the actual site, in my excitement at what I found I temporarily forgot the puzzle of the location. Sherds, some as large as four inches square, were stacked in a pile of thirty or forty fragments. And not eighteen inches away, sticking out of the rain-logged earth, protruded segments of more sherds.

Over the years it has been my policy to leave *in situ* everything that will not be damaged by the elements or risk disappearance because of its smallness. Anything I do collect, I record before moving. If possible, I take photographs.

On this day, photos were out of the question as an icy wind was driving sleet and snow out of a leaden sky. For once, careless of correct archaeological procedure, I bundled the sherds into a basket. Then scratching the surface of the ground directly beneath and around them, I uncovered more sherds, which I threw in with the first. Finally, chilled to the marrow but jubilant at my find, I went back to the jeep and stowed the basket of sherds under the seat. Then I set out across the creek to see if the north bank would give any clue which the south bank had so adamantly denied.

Quaking aspen line the banks of Skull Creek. Availing myself of a fallen tree trunk, I navigated the ice-fringed creek dryshod. Several summers before, on a hot August afternoon, I had found in this very same place a curiously shaped point **37** of black basalt. Its base was rounded, and the tip terminated in a spike reminiscent of a Prussian helmet of World War One. And ahead, where the ground rose steeply in a rocky bank, I had once found the remains of a tubular pipe made of red sandstone.

I stared at this bank now, wondering what other secrets it contained. And as I stared, I noticed something peculiar about the way the boulders lay, not entirely naturally, but more as though they had been dug out and piled. I scrambled up the bank for a closer look, and saw that the boulders had indeed been moved by other than natural forces. There was a depression in the bank, about twenty feet in diameter, just under the top of the hill. It resembled a nest.

From the bank top I looked down, and sure enough, right beside the first depression was another nest, similar in size. They were house foundations.

I walked back along the top of the ridge, looking for more, peering over the edge to see if any were concealed in the bank. But those two seemed to be the only ones. A well-made snub-nosed white quartz scraper lay just outside the rim of the first house foundation, and on down the bank were fragments of a broken mano. There were some crude, chopper-type utensils and scattered flakes in the vicinity.

For years I had noticed a hollow in the ridge paralleling the creek in the Upper Skull Creek field. No artifacts of any kind lay near this hollow, and many times as I rode by it I had wondered whether it was made by Indians, by sheepherders, by prospectors, or even by moonshiners hiding a still. With the evidence of these two house foundations about a mile above the field, I could feel reasonably sure it too was Indian. And once I took my pottery sherds home and studied them, I might be able to hazard a guess at what kind of Indians had used the habitations and when.

I had sensed in picking up the sherds that the breaks were recent, and that I would get many of the broken pieces together. But never have I had pieces go together so easily, or in such a large percentage of the total number. For example, in the Grass Valley Tom vessel, of some five hundred sherds

38

I fitted together forty-odd to reconstruct the complete base. While I could fit a few of the remaining sherds together, by and large I had no luck reassembling the upper portions of the pot.

But with the Skull Creek vessel, piece after piece fitted. I found myself assembling it so rapidly the glue did not have time to dry. The glue was recalcitrant anyhow, as I had rinsed the clinging mud off the sherds the minute I came into the house, and the wet surfaces would not set.

But as I realized what I had, and recognized the type of pottery, I was too impatient to get it together to hold my hand until it was dry.

Pottery finds vary immensely. There are sites with a handful of widely dispersed sherds, perhaps a rim sherd or two, maybe even some base sherds. Of these, two or three fragments will be found to fit together at the place of breakage.

Very different are the rare finds with a concentration of sherds, quite obviously representing a complete, or partially complete, vessel. The first such find I made was at the Dead Pile site. This was a vessel curiously decorated all over its body. It had been made by coiling. The lines of coil had been smoothed away on the inside, but on the outside they had been smoothed and then re-emphasized with an incised line. The resultant pattern has been described elsewhere as "spiral groove." This Skull Creek vessel had a similar decoration. Its type of paste, temper, hardness, and thickness were almost exactly like the Dead Pile pot.

I had never found enough of the base of the Dead Pile pot to be absolutely sure, but from the one or two small basal sherds recovered at the site, I had deduced it was a flat-bottomed vessel and might be presumed to be Shoshonean.

As I worked on the Skull Creek vessel, I found over a dozen plain rim sherds. As I fitted together the body and rim pieces, I could see I was working with two large sections of a vessel about twelve inches high. One section was fan shaped, spreading from a bottom portion about two inches wide to a rim some seven or eight inches long. The other section was roughly Z shaped, and it too went from the rim to the base. **39**

But I had no recognizable base sherds. One rim sherd puzzled me. Unlike any of the others, all of which terminated in a narrow, smoothly rounded top, this piece was flattened to a width of over half an inch. As I looked at it, I began to wonder if, instead of being a flattened rim, it could have come from the basal flange of a flat bottom.

My curiosity had to wait until the following day when I could get away to drive my jeep up Skull Creek. The weather was fouler than ever, but I did not give it a thought as I stopped the jeep and hurried directly to the inverted sage which marked the site.

I had picked up all the surface sherds the preceding day. Now, using an old hoof paring knife which happened to be in the jeep, I carefully furrowed the soil, not only where I had found the first surface sherds, but in a widening circle. I was rewarded by some thirty additional sherds, of which five were basal rim sherds. When I got the sherds home, washed them off and laid them out, they formed the unmistakable circle of a typical flat base, about four inches in diameter.

I returned one more time to the site, but found very little more.

I have described this recent pottery find of mine in such detail because I think it shows the wealth of related information I had accumulated over the years. And which I was able to use to enrich and interpret the cluster of earthenware sherds I found in the rain up Skull Creek.

In the years since I found the grey projectile point in the horse pasture buck brush, I have uncovered the remarkably complete evidence of a classic neolithic society inhabiting Grass Valley. What gives this discovery significance is the fact that Grass Valley is located in the "empty quarter" of Nevada, a sparsely populated, little-visited area where it was taken for granted few if any prehistoric remains existed. My discovery of pottery to the extent and in the variety in which it exists in Grass Valley has significantly changed any future archaeological estimates concerning Central Nevada prehistory.

Archaeology aside, the personal satisfactions of my work have been enormous. The days, the weeks, the months, the years I have spent in Nevada have been immeasurably happier because of what I have learned about the past of this country I love so well.

When I am working to reconstruct a shattered vessel, I sense beside mine the smooth, agile, brown fingers of the Shoshone woman who modelled the clay a hundred, a thousand, perhaps two thousand years ago. Then all the valley was filled with her people. Then sage hen strutted in the sage flats, and fat, greasy pine nuts roasted in the camp fires of the winter villages.

I have no monopoly on this wonderful world of prehistory, nor is Grass Valley the only place where the long dead may be called back to tell us how they lived their lives. But to those who would turn back the centuries, a word of caution.

Remember to deal gently with the ghosts you wake.

Chrysanthemums Among the Sage

AN ORNITHOLOGIST can tell by looking at an egg what sort of bird it will hatch. But even the best-qualified archaeologist cannot always predict what he will find when he begins to work on a site. Out of the most orthodox archaeological nest may leap, full-blown, a phoenix.

Archaeological time zones are generally consistent. From Paleolithic sites in North America will come characteristic fluted, lanceolate, and ground-stemmed points. Mesolithic or archaic sites usually have ground stone artifacts in conjunction with large, notched, or stemmed points. Neolithic or protohistoric sites have small, triangular points in conjunction with house remains, ceramics, stone structures, and trade goods. Like all generalizations, there are as many exceptions to these rules as there are rules. Intrusions occur from one horizon to another, and sites may overlap or intermingle in a multitude of puzzling and unpredictable ways.

There is a certain basic archaeological consistency which makes it possible to identify the geographical origin of an artifact as well as its period. For example, turquoise is found **41** in various parts of the world, and it is widely traded. But a turquoise figurine from Tibet would not easily be confused with an inlaid turquoise mask from Latin America. And a turquoise and lapis lazuli necklace from Egypt bears little resemblance to a Persian dagger handle inlaid with gem stones from Nishapur. Not only by their appearance, but by the areas in which they occur, certain artifacts are characteristic of certain cultures.

Following this premise, an archaeologist engaged in studying protohistoric and historic Indian villages in Central Nevada would hardly expect to find himself drawn into a study of Chinese porcelains. But in archaeology as in love, the unexpected is the expected.

From Indian village sites in Grass Valley I have recovered pale green Celadon ware bowls of exquisite purity of color and sophistication of form. I have found bowls decorated with prunus branches, with iris, with Chinese characters in blue on blue. I have found bowls of creamy white over whose surface tumble chrysanthemum flowers in shades of palest mauve and yellow, with foliage of vivid green.

These bowls were not lying around the village sites waiting for me to pick them up. They were fragmented into sherds, many of them no bigger than a daisy petal. And how I came to find them and recognize them for what they were is an amusing instance of how the eye sees only what it expects to see.

Big game hunters have told me a man may look at a tiger without seeing it. Only if he already has its form "in his eye" will he distinguish the striped body from the natural jungle vegetation surrounding it.

Perhaps this sort of oblivion is equally possible with less tangible objects. Where man looks for evil and ugliness he will see it all around him, remaining blind to qualities of valor, virtue, and beauty.

I once took my aunt to visit an archaeological site in some sandhills south of Reno. All she could see were tin cans and rubbish, which I completely failed to notice, so great was my preoccupation and pleasure in the traces of prehistoric occupancy which leaped to my eye at every turn. And so it is that man not only sees what he expects to see, he may be blind to those things he does not want to see.

Over the years I had spent many hours in the abandoned village sites at Grass Valley. My attention was all for the outlines of house foundations, the lithic remains, the occasional trade beads and bits of ornamental shell. Although there was in some of the villages, particularly those showing signs of more recent occupancy, a fair share of tin cans, harmonica blades, cast iron stoves, rusted tools, broken bottles, and crockery fragments, for me these objects simply did not exist.

And so I might have looked forever at sherds of Chinese porcelain without seeing them if George Metcalf, curator of archaeology at the Smithsonian, had not asked me whether there was any Indian earthenware pottery in Grass Valley.

"Absolutely not," I assured him. "I know every square inch of the archaeological sites in the valley, and there is no Indian pottery in any of them."

But not ten days after I talked to George, I was riding across the Austin meadow when, lying on top of an anthill, I saw four sherds of coarse grey earthenware. If four elephants had risen up in front of me, I could not have been more startled. I gathered them up, put them in a shoe box and mailed them to George for identification. Word came back from him that I had indeed found Indian pottery. "Let me know how much more you find," he wrote.

I immediately began looking for more. But not another sherd could I find. I looked high. I looked low. I disturbed ants from one end of Grass Valley to the other, and the ants retaliated by biting me with energy and imagination.

From previous experience I knew my failure to find more Indian earthenware was because I did not have it "in my eye." For instance, the smallest fragment of a broken metate leaped from the ground into my consciousness, because I knew it. The shape was familiar. But except for seeing specimens in museums, the four sherds were all the earthenware I had ever found. And how I happened to identify those four fragments **43** from the surrounding ground was, I suspect, more luck than perspicacity on my part.

But if those four sherds were in the valley, I felt certain there must be more. And there must be some way I could train myself to see it.

I began noticing the broken china and crockery around the villages and campsites. I studied the fall of sherds, and how a broken pot would wash from its point of origin. I studied the way light reflected off the slightly curved surface of a vessel fragment. Unlike stone, a body sherd was never flat. I looked at the edges of sherds. They presented a broken face, except when they were rim sherds. I picked up pieces of pottery and china off the ground and felt them between my fingers. Some were coarse and ridged. Some were glass smooth. The glass-smooth sherds were, many of them, a pale, clear green. I liked the feel of them between my finger and thumb. I began noticing how many of these pale green sherds were scattered in certain places. Idly I wondered if they might ever be put back together. And I wondered what they could have been. A cup? A dish?

And then one day I found more Indian earthenware. I found a whole heap of it, several hundred sherds in one place. And the spell was broken. I began finding Indian earthenware all over the valley. My hours of work with the lowly fragments of china had paid off. At last I had the pottery "in my eye," and everywhere I looked, it leaped from the ground that I might claim it for my own.

But I could not entirely forget the pale loveliness of the green sherds. When I found a piece I would pick it up and let it slip sweetly against my fingers. I would turn it this way and that for the light to shine on its limpid surface. And then I would casually let it fall at my feet and wander on. Sometimes I noticed the green sherds were not all of a color. Some seemed to have a sort of design. But I was not interested.

It was not until I began to try to reconstruct the mud-colored fragments of the Indian vessels I had collected that I remembered the different colors and designs on the china-ware. I thought wistfully that if the Indian stuff only had some

44

such pattern for me to follow, the jigsaw puzzle of putting the pieces together would be easier.

Then I remembered how the crockery had helped me find the Indian sherds. And I thought it might help me just as much in reconstructing them. If I could learn how to put together a vessel with an easy design, I might find some form or reason to the lumps of earthenware which were proving so resistant to my efforts to reassemble them in their original shapes.

Few types of ceramic can be so different as celadon and Shoshone wares. But my hunch that the one might help me with the other proved correct. There is a feel to worked clay, whether it be the glass-smooth hard paste of Chinese porcelain with glaze and overglaze, or the half-fired pots of neolithic man, stick-smoothed or paddle- and anvil-thinned. The product of the potter's wheel differs greatly from coiled or lump-shaped vessels, with their lopsided sag and humpy surfaces, streaked and clay slopped. But fundamentally, the differences are less than might be imagined.

In all ceramic ware, bases are uniformly thicker than rims, and the body tapers as it rises. Grain shows direction. Individual vessels own an identity. And like the young man of Kipling's poem who learned about women, I learned about Indian pottery from the porcelain sherds. And in learning, I unexpectedly and miraculously uncovered beauty. Texture, color, decoration, and shape were blended into a unity of effortless symmetry and grace that yet had about it something startlingly exotic.

The fragile Oriental bowls taking shape beneath my fingers were so incongruous to the surroundings where I found them, I could hardly bring myself to believe in their existence. The sparse sagebrush covering the ridges where the villages were located, the long meadows filled with cattle, the snow-covered mountains rimming the high valley, the wide sky, the distant horizons were all so typical of Nevada, it was hard to conceive of a Chinese intrusion, even by trade.

But as I reassembled more and more fragmented bowls, and the base marks baked in blue and orange characters gave **45** proof irrefutable of their origin, I was forced to accept the porcelain bowls as part of the cultural make-up of the Indian villages. And I began to wonder how they came to be there.

The Chinese played an important role in the early development of California and Nevada. They worked the mines and they worked the railroads.

No railroad has ever run through Grass Valley. But the Cortez silver mine was located in Mount Tenabo, at the northern end of Grass Valley, forty miles away. Simeon Wenban, my son's great-great-grandfather, had owned and operated the mine from the time of its discovery, some hundred years ago. He had worked Chinese mine labor. And I conjectured the Chinese miners might have come to Cortez from Austin, twenty-six miles to the southeast of the ranch. If this had been the case, they might have broken the trip by staying overnight at Grass Valley. But if they had, it seemed odd they would have left their eating bowls behind.

A suggestion to explain the presence of porcelain in the Indian villages was given me by Jean McElrath. Her mother grew up in Cortez, and as a young girl she used to see the Chinese funerals. There was a Chinese village and a Chinese burial ground in Cortez Canyon, below the mine. Jean's mother said the Chinese would place bowls filled with rice and other foods on the freshly dug graves of their compatriots. Then, as soon as the burial party left, the Indians, who had been hiding in the sagebrush and behind the pine and juniper trees, would swoop down on the grave and make off with the funerary meats, bowls and all.

Cortez is a long way from Grass Valley Ranch. It is difficult to conceive of grave goods being carried so far. There had to be a different explanation.

Not only were porcelain sherds found around the winter villages, there were porcelain fragments in isolated campsites all over the valley. Surely, where so many Chinese artifacts abounded, there must have been Chinese people. But if there were, their presence compounded the puzzle.

Throughout Nevada where Chinese worked they remained segregated in their own "Chinatowns." In Cortez Canyon the

Wenban house stood alone. Up the canyon was the Chinese village. Above, and entirely separate, was the Indian village. Across the canyon was the boardinghouse, the blacksmith shop, the Caucasian cemetery, and the miners' shacks where the white population lived. The nineteenth century had little concern with integration.

In Austin there is China Ridge. Lovelock had its Chinese settlement. And so it went in all the towns and mining camps, not only in Nevada but all over the West and even in New York City, three thousand miles away.

Was it only in Grass Valley the Chinese and Indian cultures mingled? And what on earth were the Chinese doing there, so far from their traditional roles as miners and railroad workers?

The Chinese had laundries, ran restaurants, cooked on ranches. But as I learned more about them, they began to crop up in all sorts of unexpected places. There was a Chinese fishing fleet off the coast of California during the gold rush days that sold their catch locally and also sent dried shrimp and abalone back to China. Chinese woodcutters worked in the High Sierra. There were Chinese sheepherders. And there were instances of intermarriage among Chinese and Indians.

Perhaps there never will be an explanation for the mysterious porcelain fragments among the sagebrush in Grass Valley, and yet the mingling of Chinese and Indian artifacts could have been quite natural and not mysterious at all.

47

PART THREE :
Austin Tales

Queen of Nevada

WHEN AUSTIN FIRST PERCHED on the precipitous sides of the canyon, when her quartz mills roared and thundered, and hundreds of mines tunneled the neighboring hills, when throngs crowded the steep streets, and at night saloons and dance-halls were packed with miners eager to toss away their money, in the arrogant days of her youth, Austin called herself "Queen of Nevada."

In those times of optimism, Austin taunted Virginia City, crying: "This is no longer the 'State of Washoe.' Her people have already enjoyed the lion's share. A new and formidable power has arisen in the State, based upon extent of territory, population, and incalculable wealth. Lander County possesses the resources of an empire."

Virginia City was a well-established mining center before ore was discovered in Reese River. Supported by California capital and surrounded by mines of fabulous and apparently inexhaustible wealth, it is no wonder that Virginia City considered Austin an upstart.

However, many prospectors left Washoe to try their fortune in the Reese River district. The new mines were largely financed by money from Europe and the Eastern states. In a short time what had been wilderness became the thriving city of Austin.

Austin claimed that she, rather than Carson City, was the logical repository for the Nevada mint. She asserted loud and long, through the pages of the *Reveille,* that her central position made her the inevitable choice for state capital. But that

Austin never made the mistake of taking herself too seriously is shown by the story of the Nevada Indian who visited San Francisco and was amazed to find it nearly as big as Austin!

Stokes Castle

TOWERS IN SPAIN, towers in China, towers on the banks of the Rhine, on the Grand Canal of Venice, in a dusty market place of Morocco . . .

One of the oldest architectural forms is the tower. Originally designed for defense, towers have since been adapted to other uses. There are watch towers, and bell towers, and towers from which the *muezzin* calls the Faithful to prayer; there are gate towers, and clock towers, and towers incorporated in castle walls and churches. Some are plain and some are ornate, some are very old and some of comparatively recent date. But one characteristic is common to all towers: they are built to serve some purpose specifically suited to their high and narrow proportions. This is so integral a part of towers that no one looks at a tower without wondering why it is there.

When the Stokes family built a tower on the outskirts of Austin at the height of the Reese River mining boom, the curiosity of their neighbors was aroused. If the Stokeses had built a house, however ornate or impractical it might have been, no one would have raised a question about it. Houses are to be lived in. They may reflect the architectural vagaries of their builders without exciting a single question.

But no earthly purpose could be served by the Stokes's tower that any of the Austinites could see. From the viewpoint of a housekeeper it would be a nightmare of precipitous stairs. And judged by the aesthetic taste of the day (which ran to gingerbread trim and bow windows) it was a harsh, angular building. The Austinites christened the tower Stokes Castle. Whenever other topics of conversation were exhausted, they would speculate on how or why it had been built.

During a slump in the Austin mines the Stokes family sold the tower and left Austin. But the tower remained to puzzle and intrigue successive generations.

Conflicting legends grew up around Stokes Castle. People averred that it had been built to hide the shaft of a fabulously rich mine. More romantic natures advanced the theory that it had been built to house a beautiful maiden. And whether she had refused to live in the tower or had died behind its rocky walls, no one could say. No one could really say anything which was not purest conjecture, but that did not stop them from saying it.

As years passed, Austin's glories as a mining camp were forgotten by all save Austinites and historians. But even the most casual visitor agreed that Stokes Castle was unique. Nothing like it could be seen elsewhere in Nevada. It became Austin's claim to fame. Stokes Castle appeared on tourist maps, in guidebooks, on postcards, in advertisements for gambling casinos: it had become a state monument.

But why was it built?

53

The true reason is not sensational. No hidden treasure. No lovelorn maiden. But it has a fanciful charm not to be found in those reasons supplied by idle conjecture.

In the Stokes house in the East hung a painting of a tower. The scene depicted the Roman Campagna, that flowering plain which surrounds the ancient city of Rome. Beneath a stone tower were gathered ladies and gentlemen of the Italian nobility, mounted on horseback and prepared to ride to hounds. This painting hung in Mr. Stokes's library, and the Stokes children would gaze spellbound at the gaily dressed lords and ladies curvetting on sleek horses under the lichened walls of the old tower. When the Stokeses built in Nevada, they remembered the Roman tower that had captured their youthful imaginations. The tower which they built overlooking Reese River was a replica of the tower that hung in their father's library.

Writing to me of Stokes Castle, Graham Phelps Stokes spoke of the view from the tower. "I can remember," he wrote, "the view from the balcony . . . " Many other things must have been associated with his memories of the tower; the wild, glad days of the Austin boom; the ore trucks creaking and groaning across the Reese River Valley, following a road which wound westward toward Railroad Pass; the sun sinking to rest beyond Ione. And the earliest, oldest memory of all; a small boy lifting his chin to gaze with the fixed, dreamful stare of childhood at a painting of a tower.

Building Saint George's Church

IN GAS-LIT DANCE HALLS the hurdy-gurdy girls sang their songs of dubious pleasure; from every saloon reverberated the clash of free-for-all fights, ferocious oaths, and the crack of six-shooters; and it was told of Nevada that in winter when feed got scarce the burros of the prospectors lived on the discarded playing cards which they picked up in the streets of the mining camps.

Virtually none of the hordes of silver seekers who poured into Nevada Territory in 1859 had any intention of remaining there. They came to wrest a fortune from the earth, and the quicker they could leave this country of barren mountains and burning flats the better it would suit them. There was no permanence in the houses they built. Most of them lived in tents or dugouts, and when the ore in a district was mined out, the tents would be struck, the dugouts abandoned, and overnight what had been a riotous settlement would cease to exist, as did Lander City, Washington Canyon, and hundreds of others.

To the miners, one day was like another and nobody cared whether it was Sunday or Wednesday; the stores were always open, and so were the gambling halls. Men worked and played seven days in the week and there was no time for rest.

Of the eleven years which Bishop Whitaker had devoted to missionary work in Nevada he said, "They have been years of almost unremitting labor, much of which has been attended with manifold discouragements and apparently meager results."

The bishop was loved by his flock, and he did not mind a life of hardship. It was a familiar sight to see him of a Sunday charging at breakneck speed astride a pony-express horse as he raced from Virginia City to Gold Hill or Carson City to hold services in one of his churches. If Bishop Whitaker could despair of the regeneracy of the Nevadans to whom he was devoted and among whom he had spent many years, it is easy to understand the fury of the Reverend Mr. Richardson who asked, in a report to the California Bible Society, for whom he was an agent, "Is there a State in our whole Union where there is so little religious restraint, such ignorance of the Bible, such flaunting at its teachings, such Sabbath-breaking, such heaven-daring profanity, such common drunkenness, and such glorying in shame—in short, is there another State where people so generally feel as though they were almost or quite out of God's moral jurisdiction?"

If Nevadans were lax in observing the formalities of religion, they more than made up for it by kind-hearted deeds, **55** of which the town of Austin can furnish many examples. The story of Gridley's sack of flour, auctioned again and again until it raised over a quarter million dollars for the Sanitary Fund, made the name of Austin a synonym for charity all over America.

Less well known than the sack of flour is the Buel Shoe Fund. Austin needed money to build a public school, and to raise the required sum Colonel Dave Buel offered a pair of his shoes at auction. The colonel was a popular figure in Lander County, and his size was legendary. Not only was he six feet four inches tall with a proportionate girth, but his feet were the largest in Central Nevada. The bidding at the auction was lively; the shoes were sold and resold until enough money had been given to start building the school.

The services of the Episcopal Church had been held for a number of years at the Austin courthouse. Ground had been bought and a site graded for a church, but that was as far as the matter had gone. At the Easter Service, the Reverend Blackiston announced that the collection for the day would be used toward building a church. On the plate would be a paper on which members of the congregation could write whatever sum they cared to donate.

When the Reverend looked at the paper there was a pleasant surprise. Allen Curtis, superintendent of the Manhattan Mine, had pledged himself to pay for the church building, provided that others would donate the furnishings.

Two other Austin gentlemen agreed to give the bell. Thanks to that one collection it was possible to build the Church of Saint George and also a rectory.

One of the most beautiful churches in Nevada, Saint George's still stands as a testimonial to the spontaneous generosity of Austin.

The Methodist Mining Company

56 THE FIRST SERMON preached in the Reese River mines was delivered in a saloon by the Reverend Mr. Blakely, a Methodist minister. Mr. Blakely held service in Mr. Johnson's saloon in Clifton. The *Reveille* describes how the "terrestrial spirits" were covered with a cloth so that the sight of bottles of whiskey and brandy would not offend the "heavenly spirits."

Mr. Blakely did not remain long in the neighborhood of Austin. He went to Carson City where he became chaplain of the legislature and predecessor to that outspoken chaplain, the Reverend Mr. McGrath. During Mr. McGrath's chaplainship, one of the representatives—a miner—was heard to say, "Why do they waste our time every morning with those fool prayers? If only the prayers did some good, like softening the rock in my tunnel or bringing more water to my ditch, I wouldn't mind listening to them." The next morning the members of the state legislature were startled with the following prayer:

"Oh Lord: we pray Thee to remember Representative ——. Make the rock in his tunnel as soft as his head and the water in his ditch as abundant as the whiskey he daily drinks."

A number of other gentlemen of the clergy came to Reese River after Mr. Blakely, but if the *Reveille* can be believed, they were more interested in ledges and lodes than in the immortal souls of the citizens of Lander County.

When the Methodist Church sent the Reverend Mr. Trefren to Austin in 1866, mining speculation was at its wildest. Everybody owned mines valued at thousands of dollars per foot, and nobody had any cash. Mr. Trefren had the laudable ambition to build a church. When he asked for donations from his congregation, the potential millionaires of Reese River inundated him with gifts of shares in ledges, claims, and mines.

Unfortunately the stock would not buy a single copy of the *Reese River Reveille*—let alone build a church—unless it could be converted into currency. Mr. Trefren, with rare business acumen, merged his stock and formed the Methodist Mining Company with himself as president.

Mr. Trefren was a native of New Hampshire. Boarding an eastbound stagecoach, the reverend stock promoter journeyed as fast as he could to New England.

57

What a picture he painted for his brother pastors of his
Nevada silver mines! Specimens of bromides, hornblendes,
sulphurets, and chlorides were displayed on the dining-room
tables of Methodist parsonages from Connecticut to Ver-
mont. Bewildered by Mr. Trefren's talk of drifts and dips and
deposits, dazzled by dreams of wealth, the faithful bought. As
Mr. Trefren pointed out, not only could they make themselves rich, but at the same time they were helping the church;
the Methodist Mining Company would pay dividends in
heaven as well as on earth.

So cleverly did Mr. Trefren unload his stock that there was
a boom. The Methodist Mining Company sold over $250,000
worth of shares.

Back to Austin hurried Mr. Trefren to build the biggest,
best, and most expensive Methodist church in the State of
Nevada.

Unfortunately Mr. Trefren had sold his stock at margin,
and before the church was entirely paid for, the clergymen in
New England realized they had been buying wildcat. The
Methodist Mining Company collapsed, leaving the church
with a debt of $6,000.

Poor Mr. Trefren's era of financial success was ended. The
church property was sold to Lander County for a courthouse,
and Mr. Trefren left Nevada, never to return.

In time the Methodist church was bought back, and the
debt incurred by the failure of its mining company was paid.
But the Methodist Church has never again attained such prosperity in Austin as in the days when Mr. Trefren sold his
reverend brethren $250,000 worth of shares in the Methodist
Mining Company.

The Fourth of July

"AFTER THE ORATION at the pavilion the whole crowd re-
paired to the track . . ." So says the *Reese River Reveille*, report-

ing a day of horse racing and general festivity on the Fourth of July in 1863. In those days Austin, although not as large as it was shortly to become, was already a city. We can imagine the crowd of citizens dressed in their holiday best, listening to the speeches at the pavilion and then trooping down the canyon half a mile to the Jacobsville racetrack. Overhead the sky would be a bold, bright blue, the warm air would be fragrant with sage, juniper, and the sweet wild rose, the merry voices of the crowd sounding gaily as they approached the scene of the coming race.

Wash Jacobs's track was frequently used for match races and scrub races, but this race was a special affair. A Mr. Harrington had advertised in the *Reveille* several days before that he would race his saddle horse, Red Buck, against any Lander County horse for the sum of one hundred dollars. The challenge was accepted and raised to two hundred dollars by Mr. Sewell, who leased Wash Jacobs's black gelding, Billy Adams, for the race. Billy Adams was well known in Austin as a fast horse, and Mr. Sewell had engaged the popular Jimmy Peoples to ride him. In time Jimmy was to become embroiled in some mining difficulty and to leave Austin, but on that sunlit July Fourth he was at the height of his glory. Mounted on Billy Adams he was already on the track, waving to his friends, exchanging greetings and banter.

It was not long before everybody was gathered, waiting for the race to start. Then Mr. Harrington rode up on his magnificent Red Buck. The crowd eyed him admiringly, but their heart was with little Jimmy Peoples and his trusty black.

The distance for the race was to be six hundred yards. After a false start or two, they were off in earnest. With a leap Mr. Harrington and Red Buck broke on top, but Jimmy encouraged Billy Adams with whip and spur. To wild cheers from the Austin crowd, Billy Adams caught and passed the red horse in the first hundred yards. He went on to win by a margin of fifty feet.

More races were held that afternoon. To quote again from the *Reveille*, "the day passed off quietly, everyone present having their fill of sport and whiskey."

Myron Angel in Smoky Valley

A PLUMP YOUNG MAN, astraddle of an old white plug, ambled slowly down Smoky Valley one warm spring morning in February of 1864. His hat was shoved back on his head, he lolled comfortably in the saddle. A tuneless whistle floated from his lips. The young man's thoughts were far away. He was thinking of his home in the East, of rides he had taken through the thickly wooded Alleghenies, of the Blue Ridge Mountains where the laurel and rhododendron bloom, of the Catskills with their legends and their charming valleys, where white villages nestle among green meadows, where the apple orchards shake their pink blossoms on a gentle breeze, and where church spires soar into a mild, blue sky . . .

The white horse stumbled, bringing the young man sharply back to the present—to the ferocious crags of the Toiyabe Range, tumbling southward down the flank of the grey valley, until distance dimmed their jagged peaks, and the farthest floated like a puff of smoke above the shimmering levels of a mirage. With no sign of visible regret at having his daydream interrupted, he eagerly scanned the horizon, looking for the little mining camp of Geneva, which was to be the first of a series of stops he planned to make. Already his active and imaginative mind seized on the new subject. He began to compare the mining towns of his youth, half fancying a resemblance between the secluded nooks and sunlit canyons of the Toiyabe and those distant hills and valleys of his boyhood. He thought of the camps he had known, where the raw earth disgorged its treasure of silver and gold, where the reckless, hard-working miners tossed their gold dust on saloon bars from Poker Flat to Aurora, where the mountain torrents rushed through sluice and rocker; the mining camps where miners lived in tents and dugouts, and their diet consisted of saleratus biscuits and rotgut whiskey . . .

Since the gold rush days of '49, this plump young man with the serene face and friendly eyes had been familiar with the turbulent West Coast life. His name was Myron Angel, and he was traveling down Smoky Valley as special correspondent for the *Reese River Reveille* of Austin, Nevada.

Myron Angel came to California in company with his older brother, Eugene. Eugene had been practicing law in Peoria, Illinois, when word was received of the discovery of gold on the Pacific Coast. He sent word to Myron, who was a cadet at West Point. Myron resigned from college, and the Angel brothers started West in company with the Peoria Pioneers.

Although Eugene had been practicing law and Myron studying to be a soldier, they had been brought up in the environment of a newspaper office. Their father, William Angel, had established a paper in their home town of Oneonta, New York. Once in the West, after a variety of not too successful mining enterprises, Myron took over the editorship of a Placerville, California, semi-weekly. Eugene embarked on a business venture with his lifelong friend, Mahlon Fairchild.

Shortly after arriving in Nevada, in 1860, Eugene was killed in the Battle of Pyramid Lake. The death of Eugene affected Myron deeply, and his writings reflected the hatred which he felt toward all Indians.

At the outbreak of the Civil War, Myron was glad to offer his services to Governor Downey of California, who commissioned him a captain of infantry. But the general incompetence of the state's management of military affairs eventually discouraged him. After spending large sums of his own money to equip recruits and provide food, Myron resigned to take care of his mining concerns.

These brought him to the Reese River district in Nevada Territory, where he found the two younger Fairchild brothers working as journeymen printers for William C. Phillips, the pioneer owner of the *Reese River Reveille*. Father Fairchild had been an old newspaperman. He once managed William Angel's Oneonta newspaper for him. He was the father of nine sons, seven of whom became printers. O. L. C. Fairchild and **61**

Joseph Depuy Fairchild were the two that Myron Angel found in Austin.

When ill health forced Phillips to give up his paper and leave Austin, the Fairchild boys bought him out. Soon Myron, whose mining activities were not remunerative, was working for them as editor-in-chief of the *Reveille.*

Riding toward the mining camp of Geneva, Myron met a number of people on the road to Bunker Hill and San Antonio. This is interesting because, only two months after Myron's trip, Judge J. H. Ralston wandered to his death down the same valley. In his long and ghastly rovings, not one human being did the judge encounter until he finally died of starvation and exposure below San Antonio, in what was later named the Ralston Desert. In view of the number of prospectors known to have been in the country at the time he traversed it, his prolonged agony and eventual death are not only horrible but inexplicable. However, the death of the judge, and the story of how his gold-rimmed glasses came to be buried with full Masonic honors in the Austin cemetery will have to be told another time.

Myron sent a meticulous report back to the *Reveille,* covering the mines at Geneva and the developments at Kingston and Newtonville. He had no adventures of unusual interest until he reached the Bunker Hill district, where he found the camp in a state of excitement over a boundary dispute with the Summit mining district. There had been hard feeling and unpleasantness over claim jumping, and it was determined to call a meeting of the miners.

At the meeting arguments raged furiously between the Bunker Hill and the Summit factions. When the short February day ended and night fell dark around them, no solution had been found to their problems. But, like the warriors of old, the battle ceased at sundown. Bunker Hill was well stocked with whiskey, and the lonely and isolated miners decided that so large a gathering should be celebrated. A huge bonfire was built, the bottle passed from hand to hand, and the voices which so recently had been raised in argument were now lifted in laughter and song. Stories of Injun fights, of perilous desert crossings, of wonderfully rich strikes, and the haunting, tantalizing tales of lost mines were told. And ever and again the songs burst forth, while thirty or forty miners joined lustily in the choruses. Firelight gleamed on the bearded faces and roughly clad figures, sending sharp shadows onto the canyon walls behind them. Glorious and resonant their voices thundered upward into a frosty, star-filled sky.

One miner, a shaggy and tremendous man, with an air of wildness and the look of a mountain man, sang a song which captured Myron Angel's fancy. Until then Myron had sat silent, a cheerful spectator. But now he pushed into the foremost ranks to join the rousing chorus of:

THE BOLD MOUNTAINEER

Oh, game to the bone is the bold mountaineer,
Whether hunting or trapping he knows not a fear.
    With his rifle so true and his keen bowie blade,
    His faithful cayuse and his Indian maid!
Though his locks are unkempt and unshaven his chin,
His eye flashes light when the battles begin;
With one thought to lost friends, then on to his duty!
He draws forth his steel to attack the Piute-y.
    With his rifle so true and his keen bowie blade,
    His faithful cayuse and his Indian maid!

He rides boldly on, though the deserts be dry,
The canyons be deep, or the mountains be high.
    With his rifle so true and his keen bowie blade,
    His faithful cayuse and his Indian maid!
From the Wind River Hills to the shores of Lake Tahoe,
From Columbia's dark streams to the red Colorado,
He knows every hill, he knows every dale,
For over them all goes the mountain man's trail.
    With his rifle so true and his keen bowie blade,
    His faithful cayuse and his Indian maid!

The long march is over, all danger is past,
And he's safely encamped in the canyon at last.
    With his rifle so true and his keen bowie blade,

63

His faithful cayuse and his Indian maid!
Though night winds blow chilly, our campfire burns
  bright,
Pass lively the flask, boys, we'll revel tonight!
Though rough is the life of the mountaineer free,
It's a home on the desert and freedom for me!
  With my rifle so true and my keen bowie blade,
  My faithful cayuse and my Indian maid!

Let us leave Myron Angel with the firelight shining on his smiling face. In later years he was to become a well-known metallurgist and editor of the most comprehensive history of early Nevada ever written. But on that February night in '64, his voice rose as loud as any to sing:

Though rough is the life of the mountaineer free,
It's a home on the desert and freedom for me!

"Wolf, Wolf": Austin's Participation in the Humboldt War

ALTHOUGH PROMINENCE is given the Battle of Pyramid Lake and the tribulations of early Nevadans with Chief Winnemucca, the Pine Nut Pickers, and other Indian affairs, little if any mention is made by historians of the Humboldt Indian War of 1865. It is hard to explain this indifference on the part of posterity because the Humboldt War has provided a record of Indian atrocities and instances of courage and romance unequalled by any other Indian affrays in this state.

The plight of settlers in Humboldt County was rendered more perilous by the fact that 1865 was a period of general Indian unrest. The United States Army was still concentrated at the Civil War battlefronts and few troops could be spared to assist the white men against the Indians.

64

Leading citizens of Humboldt wrote to Governor Blasdel describing their urgent need of protection against the "red devils." The governor, in turn, wrote for military aid to army headquarters in San Francisco, Salt Lake, and even Washington, D.C. But the ammunition and men furnished Nevada were inadequate. The Indians continued their depredations virtually unchecked.

Many eyewitnesses to Indian atrocities along the Humboldt came to Austin and shocked the town with their accounts. The *Reese River Reveille* published their stories in detail and also reprinted articles from Humboldt County newspapers. Indeed, as the atrocities multiplied and the massacres increased, Mr. Fairchild, the editor of the *Reveille,* became impassioned in his denunciation of the "unprincipled savages." A contagion of fear spread from Humboldt, and Austin was seriously infected.

While Indian outrages actually were committed in Smoky Valley, particularly in the San Antonio region, the Indians around Austin did nothing worse than steal a few head of livestock.

However, a rumor started that thousands of Indians were massed in the hills around Austin, preparing for an attack on the city itself. As Austin at that time contained three to four thousand inhabitants, this was a fair undertaking.

It is easy to laugh now at the hysteria which blinded Austin to the absurdity of its fears. At no time did Indians attack a large city; their depredations were always confined to isolated homesteads and small parties of travelers. But to the good people of Austin, every clump of willows concealed a band of ferocious redskins and the canyons overflowed with fiendish Shoshones and Paiutes.

In its distress and agitation Austin called on Governor Henry Blasdel for help.

The governor had taken a deep interest in the misfortunes of Humboldt, but Humboldt was sparsely settled and its mines did not compare with those in the vicinity of Austin. That a district of such wealth and importance should be threatened was most alarming. Not only did the governor

65

rush what troops and arms he could gather to the endangered city, he traveled there himself.

What an anticlimax it was for him to find that the threatening hordes of savages were entirely imaginary. At a powwow with local Indian chiefs, the governor found them a gentle and friendly group. After several days the powwow, that had started so solemnly, ended in an archery contest in which Governor Blasdel himself partook.

From the subsequent silence in the pages of the *Reveille* on the subject of the Indian menace, it is apparent that the governor spoke bluntly to those gentlemen of Austin whose cries of "Wolf! Wolf!" brought him dashing across the desert to their rescue.

PART FOUR:
Uncle Dave

IT SEEMS STRANGE that a man as colorful as David Buel has been overlooked by most Nevada historians. The following stories are reprinted from articles written by the author long ago for the pages of the *Reese River Reveille*. They touch on only a few of the events in the life of this remarkable and endearing man.

Uncle Dave and the Reese River Rush

WORD OF THE DISCOVERY of silver in the Reese River district spread through Nevada and California during the winter of 1862–1863. Almost at once the Reese River Rush started. Prospectors, miners, shopkeepers, gamblers, journalists, and the rest of the silver-crazed population turned their steps toward Central Nevada. On foot, on horseback, with burros and mules, in wagons, on buckboards, and by stage, alone and in caravans they came over the frozen mountains, across the mud flats and the alkali deserts in the early spring of '63. Just as the cry in the past has been "Frazer Ho!", "Kern Ho!", "Washoe Ho!", now it was "Ho! for Reese! The land of glittering bullion, the land where the pay streak waits for the pick of the honest miner!"

And what did they find when they got there, these scrambling, weary, dust-covered hordes of silver seekers? Why, they found Uncle Dave! They found the huge, shaggy-bearded Southerner, who had prospected the length and breadth of California, who knew every rock on Mount Davidson, and who had been one of the earliest to come to Reese River. Colonel Dave Buel and his friends, Fred Baker and Bill Harrington, had been in the district since October of 1862.

Everyone in Austin knows the story of William Talcott, former Pony Express rider, and the Apache boy, who stumbled on a silver ledge while hunting for some strayed stage ponies. The story has it that they promptly christened the ledge "Pony Ledge" in honor of the ponies, each of whom **69** already had four "feet" in the canyon.

William Talcott took as his partners the handful of men who happened to be in the vicinity. These consisted of the Jacobs brothers James and Wash, and a rancher called O'Neill who had a small ranch on the Truckee River, but was passing through Reese River Valley at the time the discovery was made. The Jacobs boys lived at the Overland Mail Station, six miles west of Pony Canyon. Wash held the position of division agent for the Overland Mail Company. The brothers later founded Jacobsville. Jim Jacobs was familiar with all the local Indians. He acted as Indian agent for Lander County over a period of years, and it is largely due to him that the Reese River District had so few misunderstandings with Indians. Wash Jacobs was prominent in the affairs of Jacobsville and Austin. He was the first sheriff of Lander County. Race meetings, balls, political campaigns: Wash had a hand in them all.

After taking part in the organization of the Reese River District and the locating of four mines—none of which turned out to be of value—William Talcott became the first county recorder of Lander County.

To Mr. O'Neill must go entire credit for the further development of Reese River. When he returned to his property on the Truckee, he took with him samples of Pony Canyon ores. These he showed to a Dutchman called Vanderbosch. Vanderbosch was a metallurgist of sorts and an unusually intelligent man. He recognized in the antimonial ore—consisting chiefly of copper, iron, antimony, and galena—traces of silver. He gave as his opinion, that, while the samples brought by O'Neill were not rich, there was every indication that rich ore existed in the neighborhood. Encouraged by Vanderbosch's findings O'Neill took some of his specimens to Virginia City to be assayed. The results of the assays were widely discussed and attracted a lot of attention, although nothing much was done.

Virginia City at that time was beginning to encounter the difficulties which made mining at the lower levels so hazardous an undertaking. Heat and water in the shafts, the threat of fire, and other factors combined to cause the slump of '64, which was already presaged in '62. Easy surface mining was being replaced by deep mining. Many miners were looking around for locations where it would be possible to realize a gain on their investment with a smaller outlay of capital.

Dave Buel and his friends, Harrington and Baker, were among those impressed by O'Neill's ore specimens. The three men set forth in October of 1862 to see for themselves what riches were to be found at Reese River. There had been few developments since the original discovery and location of the mines. A few more prospectors had drifted in. A tunnel called the "Highland Mary" was being dug opposite the present site of the International Hotel—although all the money connected with the tunnel was being put into it, instead of being taken out. Buel and his friends made various locations to the north of the "Pony Ledge."

In December, O'Neill returned to Reese River, bringing a party of men organized by Vanderbosch, the astute Hollander who had first guessed the potential value of the Reese River district. Vanderbosch joined forces with Dave Buel; a company was formed; and, on the nineteenth of December, the first important strike was made. It was called the "Oregon Ledge." Ten days later were located the "North Star" and the "Southern Light."

After the strike was made at the "Oregon," Vanderbosch had samples sent back to Virginia City for assay. When it was learned that the ore assayed at several thousand dollars to the ton, the excitement was instantaneous. The vein from which these specimens were sent was only three feet wide. But who cared if it was narrow, as long as it contained such concentrated riches.

Reese—the word was in every mouth—Reese—Let's go to Reese! But it was mid winter, and not even the hardiest ventured to start for the "Great East," as the Reese River district was called. The few who happened to be there remained. Andrew Veach, whose name is connected with nearly every early major mining discovery in Central Nevada, was camped that winter in the Simpson Park Range. The Jacobs boys were snug in Jacobs' Station. Two men called Marshall and Cole

71

had built themselves a cabin in Clifton near the "Highland Mary" tunnel, on which they were working. As for Vanderbosch and his party, and Uncle Dave and his friends, they camped out in open tents.

Provisions were scarce. The bitter cold kept everyone half frozen. One of Uncle Dave's favorite stories in after years was how they kept alive through the coldest weather by sleeping during the brief hours of sunlight, and racing up and down Lander Hill all night. "We'd been planning how, come spring, we'd grade a road up Lander Hill. But, by spring we found we'd already beat a fust class road with our feet, jes' a tryin' ter keep ourselves warm!"

At the first hint of warm weather, the rush was on. By the

hundred, by the thousand they came. Over two hundred teams were reported on the road at one time between Austin and Virginia City.

They were all traveling toward Austin. Stage reservations were booked weeks ahead, and speculators made fortunes buying up tickets and reselling them at profit.

The speculators did not confine themselves to exploiting stage tickets. They moved in on Reese River mines. They engineered stupendous deals in real estate. They bought and sold stock in companies which had no existence outside their fertile minds. Reese River stock was sold on the San Francisco exchange for fabulous sums.

In this frenzy of wildcatting only a few kept their heads. Most were too busy speculating in mining shares to do any actual work on their mines. Vanderbosch continued developing his mines, as Dave Buel did his. Uncle Dave erected the first stamp mill in the Reese River district, a five-stamp mill called the "California." This was in July of '63. Later in the same summer, other mills were constructed.

During that summer all was prosperity and promise around Reese River. New districts blossomed in every direction, houses were built, also hotels and restaurants, shops and gambling halls. Money was plentiful. Every hole in the ground signified fortune.

But cold weather brought sanity. and with sanity came a fearful crash in the values of Reese River stocks, both good and bad.

"We shore got hungry that winter!" Uncle Dave used to reminisce. "Times we'd git so all fired famished, we'd lay a quartz boulder on our bellies, ter fool ourselves inter thinkin' we'd et a heavy meal!"

Uncle Dave at the Hook and Ladder Ball

THE PRIZE for the finest ball given in Nevada Territory in the spring of '64 goes to Austin's Hook and Ladder Society. The **73** dance was to be held for the benefit of the fire department of the young city, and no pains were spared to make it a success. Founded December 19, 1863, under the name of the Hook, Ladder and Bucket Company, its charter members comprised the leading citizens of Lander County. The hooks, the ladders, and the buckets were made locally. But the firemen sent to San Francisco for their uniforms. Nothing as stylish had been seen before in the Reese River district. Made to order were the scarlet shirts, the black leather belts, and the glistening black fire helmets decorated with the brass insignia of the company.

Early in January, the society began to plan for the Hook and Ladder Ball. Committees were formed, consisting of a music committee, a refreshment committee, and an invitation committee. An advertisement was inserted in the pages of the *Reese River Reveille:* the Hook and Ladder Society Ball, to be held February 22nd, tickets will be ten dollars . . .

The night of the ball, the International Hotel was festooned with scarlet bunting. At the far end of the hall stood trestle tables, laden with local delicacies. Venison and sage hen from the slopes of the Toiyabes, jackrabbit pies, potato salads made from Dan Callaghan's Grass Valley potatoes, butter and cheese from the dairy herds along Willow Creek, bowls of fresh roasted pine nuts, not to mention cakes and pies and hot breads. The trestle tables sagged under the weight of the good food.

At the other end of the hall were stationed the members of the Austin Band. How they played! None could resist the rollicking rhythm of their tunes. Round spun the ladies, their party dresses whirling around them. With hop and skip and jump, the ranchers and miners bounded through the figures of the dance, their boots clumping merrily on the bare board floor.

Among the gay throng, the gayest figures of all were those of the Austin firemen. One fireman in particular was remarkable. And who was this resplendent figure whose gigantic torso was encased in the biggest, brightest shirt? Who was he whose laugh pealed out over the crowd like the deep ringing of a bell? It was Uncle Dave. Uncle Dave who spun his partner fastest, who bowed so gracefully, who emptied the pitcher of iced lemonade at a single gulp!

No man is perfect; even the best must have his faults and weaknesses. Uncle Dave was human. Obstinately, bullhead-edly, loyally, he had upheld the dishonored Democratic party throughout the days of the Civil War. As somebody remarked, "The only thing wrong with Uncle Dave's politics is that he is always on the wrong side." Because of this, the colonel never became prominent in the history of the state. It is as a private citizen that he must be remembered. And why should he ever be forgotten in Nevada? Such men are rare.

A miner of unusual business acumen—as his success with the Buel, North Star, and Diana mines testifies—Uncle Dave never forgot how to enjoy himself or how to give others a good time. His generosity was proverbial. As for his courage, Sam Davis says of him, "Colonel Dave Buel was afraid of nothing. The whole town knew his history. When they saw him the worst of them did not feel like making trouble." His honesty was a byword on the West Coast, and Ross Browne described him as "the only honest Indian agent I ever knew!"

Rough spoken and careless of dress with men, among the ladies the colonel was renowned for his courtesy and consid-erate manners. Round and round the ballroom at the Hook and Ladder Ball danced the colonel, whirling and twirling the pretty maidens and young matrons of Austin. And round and round whirled the other members of the Hook and Ladder Society.

When the festivities were at their peak, there was a thunder of drums, calling for attention. Onto the musicians' platform leaped Uncle Dave, his face glowing above the expanse of scarlet shirt which covered his broad chest.

"Ladies," said Uncle Dave, "and men of Austin. We are gathered here tonight fur the benefit of the Austin Hook and Ladder Society. The members appreciate the big turnout and the generous response. They've asked me ter tell yer that they consider it a sacred trust ter guard this city from the ravages of fire. It ain't much over a year since we put up the first building in this town. But, jes' because we ain't got a past, is no reason why we can't have a future!"

The dance raised enough money to provide for a hand-drawn fire engine. It was not long before a second fire company had been formed. Unlike the feuding firemen of Virginia City, disputes and battles had no part in the various departments of the Austin fire company. Because of this excellent teamwork, Austin has never suffered a major fire. Alone among the county seats of Nevada, she has been able to preserve intact her newspaper files, early records, and documents. For this unique heritage we may thank those lusty Austin firemen in the crimson shirts and black helmets: Uncle Dave and the Hook and Ladder boys!

Uncle Dave and the Lost Ledge

WHEN UNCLE DAVE told his friends in Austin that he was setting out to find a new route to the Colorado River, they guessed that he too was off to look for the Lost Ledge. All that winter little groups of prospectors had slipped out of town, heading south toward Death Valley. In the mining camps of the Reese River district the story of the Lost Ledge silver mine was told and retold. It was a story to fire the imagination, and to send the prospectors hurrying down the frozen canyons of the Toiyabes toward the desolate country below San Antone and Ralston's Desert.

Several years before, a train of emigrants had crossed Southern Nevada headed for San Bernardino, California. They disagreed on the route to be followed and broke up into small factions. One of these consisted of three men: Cadwallader, Farley, and Towne. Afoot, this trio wandered from the Amargosa River through the inferno of Death Valley. Crazed by thirst and heat, they dragged themselves from mirage to **76** mirage, miraculously surviving until they came to a small water hole named Last Chance Springs near Folly's Pass. Here they fell in with some of the party from whom they had previously separated. Together they made their way to California.

Cadwallader, Farley, and Towne had no clear idea where they had been. At one time they had supposed themselves in the foothills of the Panamint Mountains. Here they chanced on an outcropping of a ledge, four or five feet thick, which glittered with virgin silver. As proof of this wonderful discovery they had brought with them specimens of ore.

On reaching San Bernardino, Cadwallader joined an expedition to Sonora. Farley and Towne remained in Southern California, where they frequently spoke of their discovery. The story of the great silver ledge reached some gentlemen in Los Angeles, who had an assay made of the ore carried by Farley and Towne. The ore assayed eighty-five percent silver. An expedition immediately was organized with Farley as guide. But the party only got as far as Folly's Pass when Farley quarreled with a member of the party who shot him dead.

Without Farley it was impossible to find the ledge. The expedition returned to Los Angeles and engaged Towne to guide them. They barely got started a second time when Towne sickened of fever and died.

In despair, the party sent for Cadwallader to lead them to the silver ledge. It was not difficult to locate Cadwallader. But, unfortunately, he had become such a heavy drinker that it was impossible to sober him up enough to lead the expedition further than the nearest saloon. When Cadwallader finally became sober enough to understand what was wanted of him, he died.

The deaths of the three men who discovered the Lost Ledge did not put an end to expeditions in search of it. A military man called Lieutenant Bailey was able to convince a party that he could lead them to the Lost Ledge. He received from them, in token of their faith, seventy thousand dollars to develop the ledge. The party started ahead for the Death Valley country, expecting to be joined at Owen's Lake by Bailey. They waited some time at Owen's Lake. They may be there yet, waiting for Lieutenant Bailey, and thinking not so much of the Lost Ledge as of their lost seventy thousand dollars.

The catastrophies and mishaps attendant on the search for the Lost Ledge increased its fascination for the parties of prospectors who now came from all over California and Nevada to try their luck at finding it.

If anyone could have located the Lost Ledge, it should have been Colonel Dave Buel. His friend, Ross Browne, describes him: "Of gigantic frame, great powers of endurance, unerring sagacity, and indomitable perseverance." Browne was prejudiced in Buel's favor, but then so was everyone who knew him. If Uncle Dave had not been a southern-born Democrat at the time of the Civil War, he might easily have been the first governor of the State of Nevada.

Uncle Dave and five friends left Austin in the spring of 1864 on mule back. The town gave them a rousing send-off. "Spot the treasure, Uncle Dave!" the schoolchildren called. And, "Good luck, Colonel!" echoed after them as they rode down Pony Canyon.

Two months later Dave Buel and his friends got back to Austin. Dead were the mules on which they had ridden so gaily toward Death Valley. Dead too were their hopes of discovering the Lost Ledge. The hardships of the trip had stripped thirty-five pounds from Uncle Dave's huge frame. Thirst, heat, hostile Indians, and the haunting horror of starvation had shaken the confidence of the genial colonel. Though he used to say, afterwards, "We were on the right track. There was mineral everywhere. Not a blade of grass, not a drop of water, nothing but mineral! If the provisions had held out, we'd have found the Lost Ledge, sure!"

Uncle Dave in France

78 THE FASHIONABLE WORLD of Paris had turned out in full regalia for the Grand Prix, the great horse race of its spring season. The grandstand was crowded with the *haute monde*. The ladies wore multicolored dresses of fluttering silks and chiffons, and dainty parasols kept the rays of the April sun from their elaborate coiffures. The gentlemen were immaculate in black, with silken stocks high at their throats and top hats on their heads. Every seat in the grandstand was occupied save for one box, canopied and draped, in the exact center of the stand.

Colonel Dave Buel had landed in France some three days before. Hearing of the race meeting, he hired himself a carriage and set off to see what sort of horses the French had. When he got to Longchamps, where the meeting was being held, he looked around for a good place from which to watch the race. Peering over the heads of the crowd—for the colonel was an unusually tall man—he noticed the empty box. He strolled to it, and stepping over a silken cord which roped it off from the public, seated himself in a cushioned armchair.

He had just lit a "seegar" and was inhaling the fragrant smoke, when a young officer approached him, bowed politely, and made a speech in French. Now Dave savvied a little Spanish, picked up when he was sheriff of El Dorado County, California, in the fifties. He had learned Chinook when he was an Indian agent in Oregon. Not to mention Shoshone, Paiute, and a few cusswords in Dutch. But French was new to him.

The young officer bowed so frequently and spoke in so evidently polite although incomprehensible a manner, that Dave smiled and nodded back at him, and ended by offering him a "seegar." This seemed to startle the young man, for he disappeared abruptly.

Uncle Dave had barely time to take a gander at the crowd in the neighboring boxes, when his young friend came back, bringing with him a fellow officer. Dave greeted them affably and offered them chairs in his box. But they responded with a flood of French. They were still talking when a fanfare of bugles silenced the crowd and turned all eyes toward a smart equipage which was being drawn up the center of the track by four dashing grey horses. The carriage was an open one. In it sat a plump little man and a remarkably handsome woman. **79**

From the cheering and applause of the crowd Uncle Dave guessed that they must be important personages. He was surprised and pleased when the carriage stopped in front of his box and the lady and gentleman started to enter it. At this moment the two officers hurried forward, bowing low and pointing at Uncle Dave with some agitation. The colonel decided that they were embarrassed because they wanted to introduce him and did not know his name.

Stepping forward, with a fine bow, he said, "Howdy, sir. Howdy, ma'am. My name is Buel—Colonel Dave Buel of Austin, Nevada. At your service."

In the most charming accent imaginable the lady exclaimed, "This gentleman is American! Of course he must sit with us, must he not, my dear?"

The fat little man, who had been talking with the two officers, turned to the Colonel and gave him a friendly smile. "But of course the long American must remain in our box!" he said, "Be seated, I pray you."

After they were comfortably settled, the lady asked the colonel in what manner horse racing was conducted in America. He was not backward in telling her about the fine horses that raced in the West, particularly the unbeaten horse "Norfolk," who belonged to a Nevadan called Theodore Winters.

The lady showed a flattering interest in America. Before the afternoon was over, the colonel had even confided to her that he was in France on business connected with selling some Belmont mines.

Agreeable though his companions had been, Uncle Dave did not learn until he returned to his *pension* that evening that he had spent the afternoon with the Emperor Napoleon III and the Empress Eugenie of France.

Uncle Dave in Politics

80 RUMORS OF THE DEATH of Dave Buel persisted in Austin during the spring of 1864. It did no good for Uncle Dave's partner, Mr. Terrill, to say that Dave and his party had not been exterminated by Indians, had not died of cold in the Toiyabes, had not died of thirst in San Antone, had not died of heat in Death Valley . . . Nothing silenced the whispered reports, for Dave Buel and his little group of prospectors were long overdue.

When, on the evening of March thirtieth, a band of ragged men limped into Austin, nobody recognized the valiant colonel and his boys. It was not until the huge man with the sun-bleached beard, sunken eyes, and emaciated frame led his party into the saloon of the International Hotel and ordered drinks all around that he was recognized. Then it was cries of, "Dave! Uncle Dave! We thought you were dead, you old cuss, you!"

"Dead?" Uncle Dave's laughter rattled the glasses on the bar. "Why, they can't kill me!"

Ill-omened words. They might not be able to kill him physically, but—to quote Ross Browne's awful pun—the colonel was about to become, politically, a very dead Buel indeed.

The newly incorporated city of Austin planned to hold her first municipal elections in April, less than a month away. The Union party was strongly organized for the event. It was common knowledge that the popular merchant, Charles Holbrook, would be the Union candidate for mayor. Who could the Democrats run against him? Who, by the power of his personal magnetism, could carry the flagging Democratic party to victory?

Who? Who but Colonel Dave Buel, founder of Austin, the man who gave the town its name, the first to build a stamp mill in the Reese River district, owner of the Buel and Terrill store —which was equipped to sell anything from brandy to Balmoral skirts—charter member of the Hook and Ladder Society, president of the Pioneer Association of Reese River, and the biggest-hearted, best-loved man in Lander County!

As had been predicted, Holbrook was chosen by the Union party as its candidate for mayor, and Buel was the nominee of the Democrats.

A few nights later the Democrats held a rally. A platform was erected at the intersection of Main and Cedar streets. The Austin Band stirred all listeners with its rendition of that irresistible song of the South, "Dixie." Every foot tapped in time, every voice hummed the lilting tune, and from each chest thundered the chorus.

> Look away,
> Look away,
> Look away!

A barrel of whiskey had been set beside the platform, and drinks were distributed among the crowd, increasing the merriment and general atmosphere of enthusiasm. Speaker after speaker stepped to the front of the platform to be greeted by a round of applause. Well and nobly did they speak, and heartily did the crowd reward them. But nothing could compare to the ovation that burst from the throng when a tall figure, dressed in the rough clothes of a miner, a dilapidated, wide-brimmed hat on his head, his shirt open to expose a tremendous throat, his shaggy beard and hair bristling around his homely face, shambled to the front of the platform, rested his vast bulk on the handle of a miner's pick, raised a huge hand for silence, and said, "Boys . . .

"It's not for me ter go talkin' politics to you fellers. Yer know I'm a Southern-born Democrat, and the North and the South are fightin' each other in a cruel war. But, livin' out here, we ain't Northerners no more, and we ain't Southerners. Why, the Carson City big-wigs have fixed it so we ain't even in the United States! But I'll tell yer what we are, boys; we're Nevadans! That's what we are! And if yer a good Nevadan, yer a good American! It don't matter whether yer folks raised yer South of the Mason Dixon Line or North of it!

"I've been chosen ter run fur mayor of this town of Austin. As things go in Reese River, I've been in these parts a long time. I've watched Austin grow from nothin' but a couple of men in dugouts up Pony Canyon and the Jacobs brothers squattin' down in the flat. I've watched her grow, and I've

82

loved her, and I'm proud of her. If you elect me to be mayor of this city of Austin—which I named after my hometown back in Texas—I'll see to it that yer won't regret it. I won't let you down, and I won't let Austin down. She's growin' bigger every day. We want her ter be the kind of place whar decent citizens'll want ter live and bring up their children. We want our city ter have clean streets and good schools, and a hospital ter care fur the sick, and a bang-up fire company. We want law and order and prosperity. If you elect me mayor, I'll see that yer get it!"

The band struck up "Dixie." The crowd besieged the platform and hoisted the colonel on its shoulders. A jubilant torchlight parade marched through the streets of Austin. When the sun rose over the crests of the Toiyabes, there were still a few enthusiasts sitting along the gutters of Main Street, waving small flags and carolling,

> In Dixie Land
> I'll take my stand
> To live and die for Dixie . . .

Not to be outdone, the following evening was the scene of a great Union rally. The Austin Band, which the night before had played itself dizzy to the magic tune of "Dixie," this night sent the magnificent strains of "John Brown's Body" thundering up the canyon. Peal upon peal, the grand and solemn music rose,

> Mine eyes have seen the glory
> Of the coming of the Lord.

Only the battle hymn of the French Revolution, "The Marseillaise," can compare to it.

> He is stamping out the vineyards
> Where the grapes of wrath are stored.

Speeches . . . whiskey . . . music . . . a torchlight procession . . . The *Reveille* wrote: "The Unionists excelled."

83

And in the elections on April twenty-first, it was again the Union party which excelled. Uncle Dave and his fellow Democrats were defeated.

Uncle Dave and the Hanging Tree

IN THE LAWLESS SOCIETY of the early West, men soon learned to take law enforcement into their own hands. Vigilante committees and secret societies like the "601" were formed in California and Nevada. Often the only law was mob law, and the only judge accorded respect was Judge Lynch.

The sheriffs of those days were brave men who stood alone in their efforts to uphold peace and order. The names of many of these men are famous. Everyone has heard of "Wild Bill" Hickock. Nevada produced her share of lionhearted sheriffs. Men like A. P. K. Safford, who rarely took a prisoner alive, and old Joe Triplett who, singlehanded, captured three desperadoes wanted in Oregon for murder.

One day, when Uncle Dave Buel was sheriff of El Dorado County, California, he was taking a ride on his favorite horse. Uncle Dave liked a good horse. There was nothing he loved so well as a thoroughbred, and he never rode anything else if he could help it. The colonel enjoyed racing. There were no famous racers in his stable, but he got hold of a fast colt now and then. He would match a horse of his against a friend's horse for the pleasure of the sport, with a few dollars bet to back his entry.

Training racehorses in those days was far from being the scientific profession it has become in modern times. On the theory that what was good for man was good for beast, a generous drink of whiskey or brandy would be administered to both horse and rider before they went postward. Horses that had raced over a period of years came to depend on a swallow or two of liquor, and refused to make their best effort without it.

84

This has taken us a long way from Uncle Dave on that beautiful summer afternoon in the Sierra over a hundred years ago. It had been a hot day. Although shadows were lengthening, the mountain air was warm and aromatic with the scent of pine and cedar. The colonel hummed to himself as he rode along, and the reins lay loosely on the neck of his horse. That morning he had succeeded in capturing a notorious road agent. He had had a long search for the man, and he was pleased to have him lodged securely in the El Dorado County jail.

A feeling of content welled up within the colonel and found release in a song that boomed from his deep chest:

> It was in the bleak December,
>   Eighteen hundred fifty-four,
> That I left fair Plumas City,
>   Barnard's Diggings to explore.
> And I had a comrade with me,
>   An old sailor . . .

Buel broke off abruptly; something had alarmed his horse. He stopped to listen. From far up the three-mile grade down which he had just come he could hear a galloping horse, its feet thudding fast on the soft dust of the road.

Dismounting, he leaned against a boulder, the bridle reins over his arm and his hands on his pistols, ready for what might come. It was not long before he could see a horse and rider speeding down the road that wound, now in sunlight, now in shadow, among the tall trees of the Sierra. Almost at once the colonel recognized one of his deputy sheriffs.

Sliding his horse to a stop, the deputy flung himself off beside Uncle Dave. He was a young man of slight build. He looked like a child beside the huge frame of Dave Buel, "six foot four and muscled like a tiger."

"They broke into the jail, colonel, and they've tuk yore prisoner!" the deputy gasped.

With a roar that shook the air around him, Uncle Dave demanded, "How many of them varmints were there? **85**

Where'd they go with my man? Is he still alive?" The sheriff well knew that the mob would lynch his prisoner without ceremony.

"Seems like the hull town come arter him." The deputy mopped his forehead with a soiled hankerchief. "Must of been a hundred men or more. They stove in the doors. I tried to stop 'em but they wouldn't listen to me. They jest grabbed up that road agent, and away they went. Said they'd hang him at sundown from the hangin' tree. You know thet big live oak outside of town, where they hung them eight men the time Rogers wuz sheriff?"

Uncle Dave nodded. "I know!" he said, and there was a grim look in the eyes that usually twinkled so cheerily. He took a bottle of whiskey from his hip pocket and offered it to the deputy. "Have a smile, Johnny?" The boy accepted a swallow and handed it back. "We're about twelve miles out of town. If we're to reach that hangin' tree before dark, we'd better git up the road!" With which the colonel inserted the neck of the whiskey bottle in his horse's mouth and watched until two-thirds of the liquor was gone. Then he put the bottle to his own lips and drained it.

Throwing the empty bottle away, he started on foot at a brisk jog up the three-mile grade, with his horse trotting at his shoulder. When he reached the summit, he sprang into the saddle and set off to ride the eight remaining miles to town at a pace that left the deputy on his tired mustang far behind.

Night was falling as Uncle Dave rode into town. He cantered down the deserted main street. At the other end of it he could see lights. Soon he made out a crowd of men gathered around the large live oak known as the hanging tree. Flaming torches lit up the scene with a glare that flashed ruddily on the bearded faces of the mob and glinted on the barrels of the guns they carried. A wagon had been drawn under the tree. On it stood the road agent with the noose of a well-oiled rope around his neck. The crowd was evidently getting ready to pull the wagon out from under the man and leave him dangling, when the arrival of Uncle Dave interrupted them.

With one accord the crowd turned toward the big man and **86** leveled their guns at his heart. Undaunted, the colonel spurred his horse into the wild throng, shouting, "Let me speak to the man! He may have a message for his friends!"

In an instant he had reached the wagon and vaulted onto it from the back of his horse. With his bowie knife he severed the rope from the neck of his erstwhile prisoner. "Take my horse," he told the man. "Ride fur your life! And if I ever see you in El Dorado County again, I'll hang you myself! Now git!"

The frightened wretch scrambled into the saddle. With the flat of his hand, Uncle Dave gave the horse a slap on the rump that caused it to bound forward, scattering men to left and right.

Before the crowd could recover from its surprise, Dave Buel had backed himself against the hanging tree, and faced them with a pistol in each hand. The smokey light of the torches lit up his gigantic build, as he towered over them from the platform of the wagon. "You're under arrest!" he bellowed. "Every son of a b—— of you! And, I'll shoot the first man that moves!"

Somebody shouted an oath. From the back of the crowd rose an ugly mutter. Then, one of the men standing near the wagon let out a good-natured roar of laughter. "You beat us that time, Uncle Dave! But I'll bet you never see that horse of yours again!"

Uncle Dave grinned. In an instant the spirit of the crowd changed. There was laughter, friendly remarks, and banter. Uncle Dave put away his pistol and held up a hand for silence.

"It's been a long day, boys," he called. "What say we go back to town and I'll treat the crowd to a drink at the Magnolia Saloon!"

Uncle Dave and the Sack of Flour

WHEN THIS CRUEL WAR is over . . ." sang the freight drivers, lashing their teams up the Austin grade. "When this cruel war

is over . . ." hummed the faro dealers in the Austin saloons, sang the men prospecting along the Reese River canyons, sang the miners as they swung their picks in the shafts of the Yankee Blade, the Belle Creole, and the Union Flag. Even the names of the mines reflected the strife which, in the year 1864, threatened to rend the United States in two.

"When this cruel war is over . . ." This Civil War; this war that split the North against the South, this war whose scars we still carry despite larger and more recent wars. America has known no war so bitter as the Civil War. It was not fought against a common foe; it was fought by father against son, by brother against brother. And so, in 1864, the people of Austin, and the people all over America, sang as they worked and played, "When this cruel war is over . . ."

America was weary of fighting. On the battlefields the cemeteries stretched for miles. In ill-equipped hospitals, in barns, on the banks of blood-dyed streams lay the wounded.

The Red Cross did not yet exist. Money was being raised for a Sanitary Fund to care for the injured of both sides. On March thirty-first the *Reveille* received a circular asking that it arouse interest in Austin for donations to the Sanitary Fair, shortly to be held in St. Louis for the benefit of the Sanitary Fund. This fair was made the subject for a leading editorial. But a week later the *Reveille* wrote: "We hear nothing in response to the call made for subscriptions to the St. Louis Fair. Our citizens have, as yet, done little . . ." On April sixteenth the *Reveille* suggested that money be solicited at the time of the municipal election. "We are soon to have a charter election, the maiden election of our new city. How better, or more auspiciously, could we inaugurate our new government, than by making it a special point to do something for the benefit of the Sanitary Fund as we vote for our first city officers?"

On election day, boxes were set beside the polling booths in all the districts of Austin, to receive donations to the fund. But it was reported that their receipts totaled in all only $60. Men were too busy canvassing for their candidates to give to the Sanitary Fund. Feeling ran high. Tremendous bets were made on the outcome of the elections. Thousands of dollars in specie were put up and covered. And, the *Reveille* reported, on the day following the election all the Democrats were flat broke. It was a complete victory for the Union party; Dave Buel and the other Democratic candidates were defeated.

A bet which involved no money, but which got a lot of good-natured publicity, was made between R. C. Gridley and Dr. Herrick. Gridley was a partner in the store of Gridley, Hobart, and Jacobs, and he was, to quote the *Reveille,* "as gallant a Copperhead as ever lived"—in other words, an enthusiastic Democrat. Dr. Herrick was a Union man.

Gridley bet that if Colonel Dave Buel won the election for mayor, Dr. Herrick would have to carry, marching to the tune of "Dixie," a fifty-pound sack of flour along Main Street, from

Clifton, at the foot of Pony Canyon, to Upper Austin—a distance of over a mile. If Uncle Dave lost—as lose he did—Gridley would have to pack the flour from his store, down Main Street, all the way to Clifton, to the tune of "Old John Brown."

At ten o'clock on the morning following the elections, the town turned out to see the bet paid off. It was a glorious spring day. From a mild blue sky, a few fleecy clouds looked down on the festivities in Austin. Everyone was there. There were men on horseback, men afoot, ladies in carriages, innumerable children, a scattering of Shoshones, and, of course, the Austin Band.

Out the front door of his store stepped Mr. Gridley, carrying a fifty-pound sack of flour, gaily decorated with ribbons and small flags. A procession formed, led by the triumphant Union party officials, mounted on horses. Behind them marched Dr. Herrick, carrying Gridley's coat and cane. Next, in his shirt-sleeves, came Mr. Gridley, bearing the flour sack on his shoulder. Beside him walked his ten-year-old son, waving a Union flag. They were closely followed by the defeated Democrats, with Uncle Dave at their head. The Democrats carried two banners, a large sponge tied to a long pole, and a new broom fastened to another pole.

The crowd cheered and sang. Steam whistles in the mills all over town were blowing full blast. Down Main Street wound the parade. The band marched with them, lustily playing "Dixie." It should have been playing "John Brown," but it is small wonder that after such a strenuous week it had become confused.

When the parade reached Clifton, the leaders marched into the Bank Exchange Saloon. As many as could pushed inside to watch the ceremony of the throwing up of the sponge by the Democrats, and the handing over of the banners and the broom. It was Uncle Dave who presented the broom to the victorious Union men, headed by mayor-elect Holbrook.

The colonel was dressed for the occasion in a frock coat. His boots wore a generous layer of lamp black, and his tall figure was crowned with a resplendent stovepipe hat.

"Yer beat us, fair an' square, boys," boomed Uncle Dave,

brandishing the broom on high. "Hyar's a new broom ter help yer off ter a clean start! Don't pay too much mind ter the talk about how I would monopolize the water supply of Austin if I'd been chosen mayor. Yer won't have ter worry about water, now. Ye've got a *Hol-brook!*"

It must have been the spring sunshine; normally Uncle Dave's puns weren't as bad as that. But nobody was critical. The colonel's speech was greeted with cheers and "tigers."

After the ceremony there was such a babble of talk and laughter in the Bank Exchange Saloon that it was several minutes before anyone noticed Mr. Gridley, perched on Dave Buel's shoulder, and thumping the top of Dave's stovepipe hat as though he were pounding a drum. He was trying to attract the attention of the room.

"Yer'll have ter yell louder, Gridley!" said Dave. He let his own voice loose in a roar that caused all heads to turn toward him. "My friend hyar," Dave boosted Gridley higher on his shoulder, "has got a proposition. But, ye're all so uncommon talkative this mornin' that he can't make himself heard! Speak up, Gridley!!"

"Friends!" By this time Dave's hat had fallen to the ground, and Mr. Gridley was supporting himself with a hand twined in Dave's hair. "Both Union men and Democrats; you are equally my friends. Let us unite today for the sake of the Sanitary Fund. It has been suggested ..." Here Mr. Gridley broke off to pound the colonel affectionately on top of the head. "Suggested that we take my sack of flour back to Austin —as we've drunk up all the whiskey in Clifton—and auction it off for the benefit of the Sanitary Fund!"

Back up the canyon started the procession. This time Gridley rode on a fine horse, with the flour sack laid across the front of his saddle. The band struck up a rousing tune. And in no time the crowd had reached Grimes and Gibson's Saloon in Austin. Here they were refreshed with drinks on the house.

The auction started. A man called Wade was auctioneer. "What am I bid?" he asked. "Two hundred dollars!" was the reply. It was Gridley whose bid started the sale.

The people of Austin fell over themselves to get the bid on the sack of flour. None of the Democrats had any cash after their defeat at the elections, but lack of gold could not silence Dave Buel. He offered a relic of his days as Indian Agent at Klamath Falls, "Will yer take a note on the Injun Department fur $1,115?" But the auctioneer would not accept the bid. "Nothin' but gold, Dave!"

Dave withdrew to meditate with some companions over a glass of Grimes and Gibson's "O-be-joyful." He soon returned to the auction with an offer of a block, consisting of eight lots in Watertown. This was accepted. He promptly offered another block, this one of eight lots in Upper Austin.

The auction of the sack of flour was an unequalled success. By evening Austin had donated over $4,500 to aid the wounded of the Civil War.

Strolling homeward that evening, Uncle Dave stopped at the International, his favorite saloon, for a nightcap. The proprietor was a staunch Democrat. He and several friends began to commiserate with Dave over his recent defeat in the elections.

"Don't waste sympathy on me!" said Dave. "I ain't had so much fun since the night we caught old Cap Weare in the bear trap. Politics is the life! Why, I've a notion ter run for Gov'nor of the State of Nevada!" And he did.

With Uncle Dave at My Elbow

WHEN I DROVE from Austin to Pasadena I went by way of Reno. I stopped there for the night. Knowing how hot it would be on the Mojave desert, I planned to get an early start and cross it before mid day. At quarter to four I was called. Pale dawn was creeping into a sky laden with storm clouds. As I left Reno it began to drizzle. By the time I had passed Minden and was climbing the mountains toward Topaz Lake, the rain was beating down. It poured in rivulets along the winding, black road. And it was cold. The heater in my Ford had been disconnected for the summer, and I wore only a cotton dress. My teeth were chattering. My fingers were crisp with cold.

I stopped the car. Ducking through the pelting rain, I opened the luggage compartment. From a suitcase I snatched some warm clothes and a polo coat. Then I slammed down the cover of the compartment and jumped back into the Ford. Soon I was comfortably dressed. But when I reached for the ignition switch to start the car, it was locked. Where was the key? Where??

The key was locked in the luggage compartment, which had an automatic lock.

Five-thirty in the Sierra Nevada. Five-thirty, and not another car on the road. I curled up and prepared for a long wait. Fortunately my dog, Shippy, was with me. Her cheery presence made my predicament less alarming. I let my thoughts wander where they would and found myself thinking of Dave Buel. I wondered what Uncle Dave would have done in such a situation as mine.

In due course came the distant chug of a motor. I sprang out and scanned the long road southward, too pleased at hearing a car to analyze that its motor was pounding and gasping: hit—miss—splutter. Over a hill staggered an elderly sedan. Clouds of black smoke billowed from its dilapidated body. The disagreeable thought flashed through my mind that it might contain a drunken party returning from an all-night carousal.

"Injins, by God!" snorted Uncle Dave. Taking a swig of O-be-joyful from his ever handy flask, he reached for his trusty six-shooter . . .

What am I saying!

I cowered by the car, looking away over the mountains, and trying to pretend that I was standing on a deserted road in the pouring rain at five forty-five to admire the scenery. No luck. The sedan reeled to a lopsided stop beside me. From a broken window peered the bloated, villainous face of an unshaven man.

93

"Sir," said Uncle Dave, thrusting his reeking six-shooter in his belt and idly running his thumb along the razor edge of his bowie knife, "I plainly see yer a stranger in these parts. So, I'm jes' informin' yer that the climate of Nevada ain't healthy fur furriners. We're simple, law-abidin' folks in this state!" With which the colonel flipped his knife toward a skulking heathen, nailing the red devil to the wall of the Blood and Guts Saloon.

No! No!!

Rolling a bleary eye over the Ford, Shippy, and me, the man in the sedan snarled, "H'lo."

"H'lo," I echoed.

"Broke down?"

"Yes."

He sidled out of his car. His untied shoelaces flapped dismally on the wet road.

"We can't fix my Ford here," I squeaked, my voice rising like a frightened chipmunk's. In a rush of words I explained about the key I had locked in the luggage compartment. "If you can give me and my dog a lift to Minden I can get help there."

"Jump in," said the man. Pushing some old shirts and shoes to the floor, he made room on the front seat for me and Shippy.

"You live near here?" he asked, eyeing the dismal slopes around us.

"Near Austin," I answered. He looked blank, so I added, "That's about two hundred and fifty miles east."

The motor coughed and gasped. The retreaded tires thumped mournfully. Rain poured from the top of the car in heavy curtains of water.

"Where are you from?" I asked, more to break the gloomy silence than because I was curious.

"New Jersey."

Oh, magic word! Oh, bond! Oh, link! Oh, long lost neighbor! Though he had wandered far, my unkempt companion and his 1930 Chevrolet were natives of Hoboken—not fifty miles from where I used to live.

"Old friend," said Uncle Dave, setting his glass on the mahogany bar of the Slumgullion Saloon, and extending a cordial hand, "If ever yer out Austin way, I'll show yer what it means when Dave Buel says *Thanks!*"

And, I thanked the man from New Jersey gratefully when he set me and my dog down at the steps of the Minden Inn.

Through the considerate cooperation of the people at the inn, a mechanic was quickly located and I was able to continue on my way to California. The remainder of the trip was filled with adventure and the ghostly snap of the colonel's six-shooters. Until, with Uncle Dave at my elbow, I steered the Ford safely into Pasadena.

April Snow: An Uncle Dave Fantasy

SPRING SNOW WAS FALLING. Large flakes floated earthward through the still air. Soft and moist and melting, they clung to the mane of my horse, to the sagebrush, and to the boulders along the dry creek bed up which I rode. Ahead of me the cows moved, slowly and silently. Their hides were patched with white blankets of snow. The dogs arched their backs against the wet and hugged my horse's heels.

The clouds broke. A warm sun shone down on a world of green and white. Rising through the snow were tender spears of new grass, and little, low, dark green bushes of button sage, and bold, high shoots of death camus, colored poison green. Where the melting snow bared the ground, the earth lay moist and dark. On its surface glistened fragments of rock, broken by wind and storm during eons of time from the towering crags above.

Up we went, the cows thrusting forward with no need of driving. I stayed with them until Low Hills Spring was reached, and then I turned north, leaving the cows behind. A low pass brought me into Skull Creek. The cottonwood trees showed as yet no sign of leaf, but the creek itself flowed in all **95** the tumult of spring flood; brimming to the top of its banks, racing and leaping from rock to rill, turbulent and golden under the fleeting sunshine, black when the snow fell and the white flakes dissolved and died on its rushing waters.

Home lay below me, down the creek. Turning my back on the valley, I rode up the canyon. I let my horse idle with a slack rein while the pups and older dogs rioted and played in and out of the water. During the brief intervals of sunlight the birds sang an April chorus—meadowlark, song sparrow, blackbird, wren. The ground drank up the melting snow. Grey lichen was tinged with spring, grey-green, grey-yellow. Tiny leaves, close to the ground, indicated where wild flowers soon would bloom—lupin, larkspur, phlox, mertensia, and yellow violet.

Thinking of the flowers to come, listening to the wild singing of the birds, watching the exuberant dogs, I rode, unheeding and unaware, up Skull Creek. It was my horse that warned me. He stopped, with pricked ears and head raised, his breath blowing a danger signal through his flared nostrils. The dogs had seen it too, whatever it was. With hackles lifted, they drew close to me. Their eyes were intent on something up the canyon. They were growling softly, deep in their throats.

I had to look twice before I made out the figure of a man, an old man, seated on a rock. His shabby clothes blended with the country. Had it not been for the warning of my horse and dogs, I might have passed without noticing him. He did not move, but sat watching me with deep-set eyes. A weather-stained felt hat, shapeless and torn, drooped on his head. His hair straggled to his shoulders and mingled with his unkempt grey beard. His mud-caked clothes hung on his huge frame. Planted between his big, roughly shod feet was a miner's pick. On its handle he rested both gnarled hands.

It was his face which held my attention; those sunken eyes under majestic brows; that magnificent nose, like the beak of an eagle; those lines of determination and humor that stamped his lean, long features. There was something familiar about that face. I had seen it before. And then, in a flash as sudden and illuminating as spring sunlight between storms, recognition burst upon me.

"Dave Buel!" I cried. "Uncle Dave!"

A look of surprise and pleasure brightened the face of the man on the rock. "You know me?" he asked, and added hesitantly, as though he found my recognition hard to believe, "You really know me?"

"But of course I know you." The joy I felt in seeing him rang in my voice. "Everybody around Austin knows you, Uncle Dave. Even though you have been away a long time, we all remember you. But . . ." I faltered, and said rather vaguely, "I thought you had gone East." Which was as close as I intended to come to telling the man on the rock that I had read in a supposedly reliable book that Colonel David E. Buel had left Nevada to travel and settle in the East, that he had lived for a number of years in Missouri, and then had died and been buried in St. Louis about the turn of the century.

My horse had concluded that there was nothing to be alarmed about. He was standing quietly. The dogs approached the seated figure warily. When they got near him they wagged their tails and acted as though he were an old friend. The smaller pup, the timid one, climbed on the rock, curled herself against the old man, and confidently went to sleep. If the colonel were a ghost, the ghost was one of which animals had no fear.

"Yes, I went East." Uncle Dave corroborated my remark. "Had a notion I was gettin' too old fur Nevada. Nevada was a young man's country when I came here. And, although she war all cluttered up with womenfolk and babies and old men by the time I decided ter pull out, I thought I'd pull out anyhow and give some young cuss a chance ter make his pile. I'd made mine, and I didn't have no use fur more money nor I could spend. I war gettin' rich and fat and the fun war out of a lot of things. The family wanted ter make a splash in society, and go gallivantin' some around the country. So we took off.

97

"I've seen a lot of places since then. But there ain't never been none come up ter Pony Canyon when we struck her rich the spring of '63. Nor trips like the prospectin' trips down Smoky, past San Antone and inter that hell-fired Panamint Range. Nor gold rushes like the rush ter Eureka. Nor strikes like the last big strike I made in Belmont.

"I've been a long way since then." The old man shoved his hat back on his head and chuckled. "Young lady," he said, and his eyes twinkled. "I've been cl'ar ter Hell and back since my Nevada days. Heaven too, but it war Hell made the biggest impression.

"Went ter Hell right after they buried me in St. Louis. When I reached the gates ter the underworld, there war a man guardin' the entrance.—Hello, Jake, I says.—Who d'yer think yer talkin' to? the man says—Why, ain't you my old friend Jake Van Bokkelen what used ter be provost marshal in Virginia City? —Yer can call me Jake if yer wants to, said the man, but most people around here knows I'm the Devil!

"He let me in and we shook hands.—Where's yer pet monkey, Jake? I asks him. Van Bokkelen had a monkey went everyplace with him. I war sure the monkey'd be with him in Hell. But Van Bokkelen war busy greetin' some new arrivals. He didn't answer.

"I wandered off and began lookin' around. There war a big commotion over ter one side. I goes over. There's a team with a heavy load of ore, and the mule skinner swearin' the air blue. —Hello, Big John! I calls. The skinner looks up and waves and asks me if they've widened the Austin grade any. But he's back ter cussin' his mules before I can answer.

"It may be that war the county of Hell they put me in, but there warn't a soul down thar didn't come from Austin or Virginia City or Aurora or Eureka or Belmont and such like. There war some latecomers from a town called Tonopah.

"All we did war sit around and talk about the rich lodes we'd located, the strikes we'd made, the mines we'd lost. Bryfogle war there. We used ter drive him crazy askin' about his Lost Ledge.

98

"But I got ter thinkin' about some of my friends that warn't there; Harrington my old partner, Ross Browne the artist, and a host of others. So I went ter Jake Van Bokkelen at the gate and says—Look, Jake, I know every man in this place. But thar's a lot of my friends ain't here. If it's agreeable ter you, I'd like ter look them up. Whar's Gridley what toted the Sanitary Sack of Flour through Austin? And Bishop Whitaker who bought my good sorrel geldin'?

"Jake pulled out a big book. He hunted around until he found my name, with a heap of writin' under it. He reads a bit and then says, surprised like—Yer war an Injun agent once, warn't yer?

"I allowed that war a fact.—Whar d'yer keep Injun agents? There ain't one here.

"Jake laughs and says I'd better be glad I don't see them. They're in a much worser part of Hell, with nobody ter talk with but Injun agents and other employees of the Department of the Interior.

"Jake reads further. Then he says—Yer used ter be a sheriff too, didn't yer? And I allowed I war.

"—Where are sheriffs stabled?

"Jake laughs again and says—we scatter sheriffs. Thar's quite a bunch of them in Heaven. Maybe that's where yer'd better go if yer want ter see the rest of yer old friends.

"I war always fond of travel. So Jake writes me a pass and tells me ter give it ter Saint Peter. And off I goes.

"When I gets ter Heaven, Saint Peter looks at my pass and says—That's no good. Why, it's written by the Devil!

"I explains that I have some friends inside and I'd like ter visit with them fur a little. But Saint Peter hears I'm from Nevada and he says very, very few Nevadans go ter Heaven. —There were some newspapermen in here from Nevada, Saint Peter said. They grew so unruly, we were obliged to ask them to leave. Even Father Manogue and Bishop Whitaker are far from conventional in their behavior.

"We talked together a while. But the saint had his mind made up against Nevadans, so I said good-bye, and started back ter Hell.

99

"When I got ter Hell, Jake Van Bokkelen warn't at the gate. Instead it war another Nevadan; a man I knew well and never could abide. It war Henry G. Blasdel, first governor of Nevada and an old political enemy of mine. I ran against him in '64, in the first election fur governorship of the state. That war a hard-fought campaign. Why, some of the men that took part in it still have a hangover! I rigged up a wagon and hired a driver. Then, I got two barrels of whiskey and toured the state. Every town we reached, out would come the municipal band playin' Dixie. Thar'd be a torchlight parade—singin'—speeches—whiskey flowin' like creek water. In the end, Henry G. beat me. We never got along too well after that campaign. Henry G. took his politics more seriously than I did. He said my political platform war only a raft bobbin' on an ocean of rotgut whiskey. What I said I'd better not repeat.

"We were never friends. When Henry G. Blasdel met me at the gate, and I asked where Jake had gone—Jake's takin' a holiday said Henry G., holdin' his foot against the door.

"Well, open up and let me in, I says. It's cold out here! But Henry G. said he'd see me in Heaven before he'd open the gates of Hell fur a Southern-born Democrat like me. We argued a while, but I finally had ter go away.

"As I left, I could hear Henry G. laughin' like a moonstruck kyoti . . .

"Hell didn't want me. Heaven wouldn't take me. The only place left fur me war Limbo. Limbo is a forlorn place, somethin' like Carson Sink in a windstorm. The people in it are lost souls, too good fur Hell but not suited ter Heaven. Sagebrush Burnett's sister tends bar there. Colonel McDermit that the Injuns killed is there. And so is Jim Banks, that used ter be called the Martyr of Paradise Valley. Thar ain't nothin' wrong with the people in Limbo, but it's no place fur a man.

"We talked some about Earth in Hell; in Limbo we talked and thought of nothin' else! We war like drunks denied drink; like addicts wantin' opium. We talked day and night of Nevada, and our voices war like echoes in an abandoned mine shaft. Only there warn't neither daylight nor dark; just constant twilight, until I couldn't stand the place no longer. I made up my mind ter git up and git. And when I pulled out of Limbo, my course war laid fur Earth!

"When I reached Earth, I went straight to Belmont, Nevada. That war the last camp I helped start. But, one look at Belmont showed me I'd been gone a long, long time. There war rabbit-brush in Main Street, and what houses hadn't been carted away had fallen down. Nothin' war left but the courthouse and the cemetery!

"I shouldered my pick and struck out fur Eureka. Eureka hadn't entirely fallen ter seed like Belmont, but there war some mighty peculiar things goin' on in the town. Deep minin' with diamond drills, and all kinds of foolishness. I hung around Eureka a day or two, then I headed down the road fur Austin.

"What a road! No teams—no dust—no horsemen—nobody on foot; just a lot of things like cannonballs whizzin' by with a noise like a hungry mosquito.

"Austin warn't the camp I remembered. No crowds of miners jostling each other at the International Bar. No hurdy-gurdy girls. No six-shooters poppin' through the night. The town war dead—played out. Some Austin people talked of platinum in Lander Hill. In my time, news like that would've brung half California rarin' inter Pony Canyon. But no one showed any excitement—not what I call excitement.

"Belmont, Eureka, Austin; I founded all three towns. But when I came back ter them, all war like strange towns ter me. It made me know I'd been dead a long time. But a prospector ain't plumb dead if he's got a pick and some unclaimed country ter poke around in.

"I shouldered my pick and turned north up the Toiyabes, like I'd done many times before. Mountains don't change. They war here before us; they'll be here when the last man goes." Uncle Dave lifted his eyes to Mount Callaghan and fell into a reverie.

Never ask a ghost a question. I have learned that, but I learned too late. "Will you stay, Uncle Dave?" I asked. "Will you stay in the Toiyabes?" As I spoke there was a rush of snow —thick, dancing flakes that whirled around me and blinded **101** me completely. The flurry lasted only a minute. When it stopped, I looked at the rock where Uncle Dave had been sitting. He was gone. Only the dogs remained, huddled around its base.

Knowing it would be useless to look for footprints, I called the dogs and turned my horse toward the valley.

All the way home I thought of Colonel Dave Buel who had come back to the country he loved. I hoped that somewhere, swinging his pick that left no mark on the rock it struck, somewhere Uncle Dave would find bonanza.

PART FIVE:
Mountain Stories

Christmas Trees on the Mountain

IT SNOWED THE OTHER DAY, a soft fall of giant flakes that fell from a windless sky upon a winter world. Along the creek the willows bowed under white cloaks of snow; the sage and rabbit brush made round white mounds, inside of which lived hidden communities of birds and mice. On the undrifted reaches of snow lay fresh tracks of the wild things that went abroad for food: rabbit trails, coyote tracks, and the sharp bounding hoofprints of deer.

I saddled my horse and rode along the foothills of the Toiyabes looking for cattle that might still be outside. Hardly realizing it, I drifted higher up the sunlit slopes of the mountains, up dry canyons until I came to the first low straggling trees. Only a little further and the pine trees were all around me. Snow was heaped upon their branches and each snowflake sparkled and reflected a thousand lights; they were more beautiful than any Christmas tree decorated by human hands.

That night before I went to bed I looked long from my window toward the mountains where the pine trees grew. The sky was lit with a glitter of stars. One star, shining with particular brilliance, seemed to hang directly over the canyon where I had been riding. I thought of the Magi with their wondrous gifts, those three kings who rode across the distant desert following the radiance of a star two thousand years ago. Perhaps the Magi passed a grove of snow-garlanded evergreens as they journeyed to find the stable where lay, on the sweet-scented hay, among the cattle and the long-eared burros, our Saviour, Jesus Christ.

105

Old Sledge Preserves the Range

IT WAS A BEAUTIFUL JULY AFTERNOON. With the garden hose I was sprinkling the shrubs and flowers around the house, when a truck drove into the yard. In the truck was a house painter with his assistant. When he asked to paint the roof, I was delighted to give my permission. The house had not been touched for years, and the roof was particularly in need of paint.

It was not long before the painter had set up his apparatus, and he and his assistant were scrambling around on top of the house, spreading red paint over it and all the adjacent territory. It was disturbing to see my yellow roses mottled with red paint. I would have been even more upset at the sight if I had guessed that the first rain would wash the paint from the roof as thoroughly as though it had never been put there.

My attention was diverted from the havoc the painters were wreaking by the arrival of another car in the yard. This was a model T Ford, festooned with cooking utensils and the shovels and picks incident to a prospector's life. At the wheel sat a wisp of a man, as gnarled and twisted as a juniper tree. From beneath a frayed straw hat his grey hair fell to his shoulders. Tobacco juice mingled with the straggling whiskers that framed his toothless jaws. Blue eyes twinkled behind a tangle of eyebrows, and the skin of his face was burned black as shoe leather by long exposure to wind and sun.

Every summer this battered car made its appearance in the district and stayed until snow flew. The car was the property of a prospector called Old Sledge. Old Sledge had not confined his life to mining, although to hear him tell it, he had been at every important strike since gold was first panned on the Stanislaus. In fact there were few trades Old Sledge had not tried, few places he had not seen.

The actual facts of his past were a mystery, not from any reticence on the part of Old Sledge, but from the bewildering and contradictory profusion of his recollections. Whether his nickname of Old Sledge came from a game of chance that was popular in the early days of the West, or whether he had taken the name in honor of one of his most celebrated stories—the time he was hauling ore up Grass Valley the winter of the big snow—no one knew. As Sledge used to tell it, that winter the snowdrifts were so high he had to dig a tunnel for his mules all the way from Cortez to Austin . . .

We sat down on the porch. I had brought Old Sledge a bottle of beer, and was looking forward to a few pleasant moments in his company, when once again the white gate creaked open and the third car of the day drove up to the **107** house. It is not unusual for months to go by with no car except the ranch trucks and the weekly stage coming on the place, so all this traffic was most unexpected.

The third car had a Los Angeles license plate and was driven by a woman. Sitting with her on the front seat were a little girl and a man. The woman stepped briskly from the car and entered the garden. She radiated amiability and poise. Under a sailor hat her hair clustered in crisp curls around her well-fed face. Her protuberant eyes took in every detail of the group on the porch; Old Sledge with his bottle on a table beside him, and me dressed in Levi's and moccasins.

Introducing herself, the woman addressed her conversation entirely to me, as the lesser of two evils. "I understand this is Grass Valley ranch?" I nodded. "Well," said she, "I dropped in to tell you that I am going to be spending the rest of the summer up Skull Creek with my daughter and my cousin." She gestured airily toward the occupants of the car. "There are a number of things I want you to do for me, such as bring me my groceries and mail. Of course I shall make my phone calls from your place." The dazed look of incredulity and horror that was growing on my face caused her to ask sharply, "You do have a phone, don't you?" I nodded, speechless. "Now that that is settled," she said, "there are one or two questions I want to ask about this region. Is it safe?"

"Safe?" Still stunned by the prospect of having this woman with her family camped on my doorstep all summer, I could only ask, "What do you mean?"

"Are there any," her tone reproached me for my stupidity, "predatory beasts in those hills?" And she pointed a manicured finger in the direction of Mount Callaghan's soaring bulk.

"Why, no." I told her, racking my brains for any dangerous animals. "The gnats may bother you. And then, of course, there are ticks . . ." I had been staring out across the yard as I spoke, half hoping something might appear to rescue me from this dreadful woman, when I noticed a small swirl of dust start near the gate. Whirling rapidly, it soon increased in size, rising higher and higher, picking up small twigs and wisps of hay. Higher and higher it rose, behind the unconscious back of the lady from Los Angeles, until it was a giant dust devil. Outside the whirling spiral of dust nothing moved. There was no breath of wind to give warning before the dust devil struck the house. Away went the flimsy table, from which Old Sledge had thoughtfully rescued his bottle. Away went the sailor hat that had perched so jauntily among the curls. And, away with a fearful clatter and bang went ladders and paintbrushes and, with a despairing shriek, away into the blue sailed the painter's assistant.

I rushed around the end of the house to pick up the remains of the assistant. He had landed harmlessly, if rather suddenly, in the top of a matrimony bush. No bones were broken and he lost no time in collecting the fallen ladders and brushes and getting back on top of the roof.

I returned to the front porch to hear Old Sledge say, "Wind? Why ma'am, that warn't no wind. I recollect back at the turn of the century I had a little ranch north of here a ways. Was an uncommon windy year, and I noticed every time there'd been a big blow, some of my calves'd be missing. Finally got so I didn't have a cow with a calf left on the place. Well, I saddled up a horse, and off I rode ter call on a neighbor of mine, Sam Crow by name, who lived on the opposite side of the same mountain range as I did. Now, when I got inter Sam's meadow, dang blast if I didn't notice all his cows was nursin' twins, and there was a couple of 'em had triplets.

"I went ter the house. There was Sam a'eatin' a big veal stew. 'Sam,' I says, 'How come all yer cows has twins and two even has triplets?'

" 'Those cows didn't none of 'em have twins. Nor triplets neither,' says Sam. 'All them extry calves is leppies that kep' a'blowing' in here on windy days. Yes, sir, them calves jes' dropped, a'bellerin' and a'hollerin' out of the western sky. My cows is plum wore out a'nursin' of 'em. If I could find the man what owns 'em, I'd shore charge him plenty fur the feed them miserable leppies has cost me, and fur the way they've drug down my pore old cows!'

"Well, ma'am, yer won't believe it, but I jes' clum back in my saddle and rode home without havin' said a word ter Sam about how them calves was mine. Pretty soon the wind changes. Yer kin call me a liar, ma'am, if those calves didn't blow right back over the mountain inter my place. When Sam come a'lookin' fur 'em, there warn't nuthin' he could do but go home and pray fur a west wind!"

Without giving the lady from Los Angeles a chance to interrupt, Old Sledge continued, "Warn't yer askin' about wild beasts as might be dangerous around yer camp? I shore hope you or yer cousin is a good hand with a rifle, ma'am. The Toiyabe Range is famous fur the size and ferocity of its mountain lions. When I war a boy and more reckless nor what I might be now, I war ridin' over toward Cowboy Rest when I rode right on top of the biggest mountain lion I ever hope ter see in this life or the next. Well, I shakes out my riata and claps spurs ter my horse. Away I sets arter that lion. Across Rosebush Canyon he goes, and me behind him, a'whippin' over and under, and a'gougin' that horse in the belly as hard as I kin ride. Past Chapel Spring we races, and clear ter Sandstone Canyon, whar I gits a good throw at him. But that lion jumps inter the loop, and I got the dang brute roped around the middle and him a'roarin' and a'yowlin'. Pretty quick he turns and takes to me. Then I'm a'ridin' even harder ter git away from him than I was ter ketch him. Back we comes out of Sandstone Canyon, and past that Chapel Spring we tears. I don't have ter whip and spur none; my horse is as anxious as me ter keep the lead. About the time I gits across Rosebush, I figgers I don't need that riata no more, and I turns the lion loose. Even arter he got loose, he chased me clear ter Cowboy Rest. I could hear him a'paddin' and a'snufflin' round the cabin all night long.

"But the wild beasts ain't nuthin' bad, ma'am. It's the lightnin' yer should watch fur. Many's the time I've rode up Skull Creek a'dodgin' lightnin' like a kid dodges apples in an orchard. Reminds me of the time . . ."

An ear-splitting shriek from the lady from Los Angeles put an end to that particular recollection. Our pet bull snake, who

110

lives under the house, had chosen that moment to come out and sun himself.

"That snake!" quavered the lady. "Is it a rattlesnake?"

Before I could reassure her that it was a totally harmless variety of reptile, Old Sledge broke in. "Why shore, ma'am, that thar's a rattler."

"Shouldn't he have rattled to warn us of his approach?" she asked.

Old Sledge peered at the bull snake's smooth tail for a minute, then he said, "Them rattles gits mighty agrivatin', ma'am. So these folks whacks 'em off when their rattlers is little fellers—like choppin' off puppies' tails."

Without another word the lady from Los Angeles fled to her car and drove wildly off in the direction of California.

"Sledge!" I said accusingly. "What ever possessed you to tell those awful stories to that poor woman?"

Old Sledge savored a swallow of beer. "Why, couldn't yer see what I was a'doin'?" he said. "I was a'preservin' the range!"

Double Trouble

TOWNS, LIKE PEOPLE, have personalities. And word gets around among the gentry of the open road which ones to avoid, and which ones will greet the weary traveler with a friendly word and a helping hand. Surely the town of Austin belongs in this latter category, and for this reason it is more than strange there is never a gypsy seen there, nor has been in twenty years.

At one time gypsy caravans were common, and it was nothing unusual to hear the halting motors of their overloaded cars, driven by dark, cutthroat men, as they struggled up the steep grade into town. Out of every crack and opening hung bright-eyed gypsy children with uncombed hair and flashing

111

smiles. Aloof and mysterious beside the saturnine men and restless children sat the gypsy women, dressed gaudy-gay in sunset colors.

Sheriff Hammond always worried when the gypsies came through Austin. Their fingers were light for silver-mounted headstalls and bits. Their eyes were quick to spot a straying chicken, plump and ready for the pot.

But the townspeople loved to see the gypsies come. The Austin children stared, round eyed, at the lean, wild, carefree, wicked gypsy boys and girls. And the Austin women drew close around the gypsy women wanting their fortunes told, wanting to hear again, and yet again, the romantic, never-realized tale of a wealthy stranger who would carry them far away on a long sea voyage.

Why did the gypsies stop coming to Austin?

The great, transcontinental Highway Fifty in its route across Nevada bisects the town. Piñon-covered slopes make an ideal campsite for travelers who like to sleep under the stars. The gentle, isolated little town of Austin would seem to be the realization of a gypsy's dream. Why, then, do they now avoid it? What happened?

I never knew, until one day I heard the story of Slim Maine, and how he out-gypsied the gypsies.

Slim was a railroad man from Arkansas. He happened into Austin one day on the old narrow gauge. Tall and thin, a man who would rather lean than stand, lie than lean, Slim had a slow, nasal voice like an ungreased hinge.

He got off the train at Austin. The reason he got off was not that he wanted to see Austin. It was simply that Austin was the end of the line. And having got off the train, he somehow never got around to getting back on and leaving.

In Austin he met an Indian maiden called Amy. She did all she could to make Slim feel at home. And so successful was she, that he married her.

Amy was an heiress. Her father's family had been living around Austin for two thousand years. And her father, Chief Toi Toi, had a bit of property some forty miles north of Austin known as Cowboy Rest. The restful name no doubt appealed to travel-weary Slim. And it was there Slim and Amy settled. Amy was a hard worker and a wonderful cook. Slim was a big eater and rested a lot. Both were happy at Cowboy Rest, each in his own way, although by one of the ironies of life, the harder Amy worked the fatter she grew, while Slim stayed skinny as a bull snake in spring.

He usually put in some time in the hay fields of one of the Grass Valley ranches during the summer, to lay in enough cash to buy the winter's supply of groceries for himself and Amy and their growing band of children.

It so happened that on one of Slim's annual shopping trips to Austin with Amy and the kids, a gypsy caravan arrived in Austin too.

Slim parked his car in front of the International Hotel. Out spilled his kids, whooping with excitement. They scattered like young sage hens up the canyon. Amy stepped out, smoothing down her starched cotton, and waited placidly while Slim unfolded his emaciated length from behind the steering wheel. He took his frayed wallet from the hip pocket of his faded Levi's and slowly counted out seven ten-dollar bills.

"Here," he said. "And don't go buying any of that new-fangled stuff, like canned tomatoes."

He handed the money to Amy.

"Seventy dollars don't buy much," she said, looking wistfully at the folding money that remained in the billfold Slim was putting back in his pocket.

"We don't need much," said Slim. "Sugar. Flour. Coffee. Maybe a side of bacon. Holler when you got the stuff together and I'll help tote it to the car." With that he disappeared into the International to see if there might be a game of poker which he could join.

The bills held in her hand, Amy started toward Honk Francis's general store. She had taken only a step or two when a lean gypsy woman appeared from nowhere and fell in beside her.

"Your fortune, pretty lady," crooned the gypsy. "Cross my palm with silver. Let me tell your fortune."

Amy shook her head. Her mind was on the groceries she was going to buy.

113

"I see a tall stranger in your life," insinuated the gypsy, speaking husky sweet.

Amy giggled. "That's Slim," she said, and kept right on walking toward the store.

"I know your life. I see your future. Let me read . . ."

Amy pushed by. "My life is groceries," she said. "Four kids and a man to buy for, and not enough money to buy with. If you think I got silver to spare to hear a fortune I already know, you ain't got no idea the price of flour in Austin!"

The gypsy sprang in front of Amy, barring her way. They were about the same height, but while Amy was long bodied, short legged, with a round, rosy face and merry, slitted eyes, the sinuous gypsy woman seemed to balance to unheard music on her long, dancer limbs. A lurid, orange satin skirt swathed her narrow hips and swirled in ruffles over her bare feet. A dirty white blouse slid off one naked shoulder. And her long, black hair tangled itself among the gold hoop earrings in her ears and tousled over her hungry eyes.

Instinctively, Amy drew back from the wild woman, then planted herself stolidly, the laughter draining from her face and leaving it heavy and blank. "What you want? Why you stop me?"

"Pretty lady," placated the gypsy, and lashed lids concealed the saurian glitter of her eyes. "If you need money, let the gypsy woman help you. Let the gypsy woman say the gypsy spell, and double your wealth. Where there was one golden coin, there will be two. For fifty dollars, one hundred."

Amy tightened her grip on her seven ten-dollar bills. "What you talking about? That's crazy talk!"

"Nothing is crazy for a gypsy. Nothing is impossible. Give me your money to hold while I say the gypsy spell, and I will double it for you."

Fascinated in spite of herself, Amy stared at the green bills. Her fingers unclenched and she fanned the money, looking from it to the gypsy and back again. "Double . . ." she murmured. "Twice seventy is a hundred and forty." Amy could neither read nor write, but she had mastered arithmetic instinctively, as a bird learns to fly. "A hundred and forty dollars

114

is money enough to buy candy for the kids. And store soap. And canned tomatoes." She shook her head. "Crazy!" And she crumpled the bills in her fist. Fiercely she confronted the gypsy woman. "Why you talk such nonsense?" she shouted.

"Because it's true," whispered the woman. "You've seen, on a clear day, one little cloud show on the horizon. Soon comes another cloud. And another. Until all the sky is covered with clouds. Money is like clouds, and one dollar breeds more dollars. You've noticed the clouds, haven't you? You know I speak true."

"What do you take for your share if you double my money?" Amy asked. She had had experience with bankers, and knew money never came for free.

"Nothing," said the gypsy, speaking boldly, for she sensed victory. But need breeds caution, and she saw still a trace of suspicion in the Indian woman's face, and so she waited to make sure, explaining, "When I double your money, it will work for me too. What do you care if I make a few dollars, so long as you get back twice what you gave me?" She held out her strong, slender hand. "Give it to me!" she commanded.

But Amy gripped her money tighter than ever. "Why give it to you?" Amy's need was as great as the gypsy's and in her veins ran the blood of Shoshone chieftains, wily in war, skilled in the arts of ambush, trackers of game, defenders of their hearths. "It's my money," said Amy. "If you can do what you say you can, double it for me while I hold it."

The husky voice fell low and grieving. "Too bad. The gypsy spell works only if the money is in my hands."

"You'll give it back, if I let you hold it?"

"I'll give it back, *double.*"

Reluctantly, hesitantly, Amy held out her seventy dollars. And swift as a hawk falling on its prey, the gypsy woman snatched it, spun on her bare heel, flame-orange skirts arcing around her, and set off up the street with long, swinging strides.

"Wait! Wait!" cried Amy, as she saw the woman with her money streaking up the canyon. But the gypsy did not so much as turn her head.

A black, dust-coated car pulled to the curb beside her. She flung herself inside. Amy had a momentary glimpse of dark, mocking faces laughing at her as she waddled up the road in helpless pursuit. Then the car rounded a steep bend and disappeared into the mountains.

A little group gathered around Amy. They listened sympathetically while the daughter of Chief Toi Toi wept aloud. "What'll I do?" she wailed. "Slim'll kill me when he finds out I've lost the grocery money. Our whole winter supply of grub! And I let that gypsy run off with it. I said she was crazy. I was the crazy one. Loony crazy! Oh, Slim'll kill me, sure!"

The sheriff, Frank Hammond, joined the group. After listening a minute, he began to question Amy. As soon as he could make out from her incoherent laments what had happened, he said, "I know that gang of gypsies. I'll call Eureka to put up a roadblock and stop them if they get that far. And I'll start after them right now in my car. You find Slim, and wait for me with him at the courthouse. How much of your money did that woman take?"

"All I had!" and Amy wept to tell it.

Hardly an hour later Sheriff Hammond was back at his office, herding the gypsies in front of him. There were nearly a dozen, young women and old, several swarthy men, children of every imaginable size and age.

"Is the woman here who took your money?" Sheriff Hammond asked Amy.

Her first paroxysm of grief over, Amy had sunk into a lethargy of woe. Sitting beside her, Slim seemed to be dozing, but a gleam under his closed lids showed he was missing nothing that went on.

Mutely, Amy pointed out the woman who had robbed her. She was the handsomest one of the lot. Her long hair had tumbled down her back, and she tossed it with a proud, angry gesture as she furiously denied ever having laid eyes on Amy before in her life.

"I've known Amy a long time." Sheriff Hammond said to the gypsy. "If she tells me you robbed her of her grocery money, I believe her. Amy, how much money did this gypsy take?"

"I took nothing!" screamed the gypsy. "If the squaw says I robbed her, she lies! What money I have of hers she gave me, of her own free will. A few dollars. She gave them to me to make a gypsy spell. I stole nothing! It's the truth."

"How much was it?" Sheriff Hammond again asked Amy. And when she still sat mute, huddled on the bench like a sack of old clothes, he turned to Slim. "How much did you give your wife, Slim?"

Slim had a hunk of tobacco in his mouth. Deliberately he shifted it from side to side, and shot an amber stream in the general direction of a spittoon before he answered.

"Wal, Frank," he drawled. "It war my whole summer's earnin's I gave Amy to buy the winter's groceries. It waren't much, but it meant a heap to us. Amy tells me the gypsy woman promised to double it. Did you?" he shot at the gypsy.

She looked insolently down on him, hand on hip. "Did I what?"

"Did you promise to double Amy's money?"

"I promised nothing! The few pennies your wife gave me were for a spell to rid her of an unloved husband."

"Reckon it war quite a spell," said Slim. "Amy here tells me it cost her one hundred and forty dollars."

"What! The squaw gave me seventy. Not a penny more!"

"So, you admit you took money from her!" crowed Slim.

The gypsy shrugged defeat, pulled a crumpled handful of bills from the bodice of her flimsy blouse, and threw them on the sheriff's desk. "There's your wife's money," she snarled.

Deliberately Slim counted the seven ten-dollar bills. "Ain't but half here," he said to Sheriff Hammond. "One forty war the sum."

And one hundred and forty dollars did the gypsies pay before the sheriff let them go.

Driving home to Cowboy Rest that night, the kids sleeping pell-mell among the sacks of staples and cartons of tomatoes, Slim glanced again and again at Amy, sitting glum beside him. Finally he said, "What's wrong?"

"I'm worried about that gypsy woman, Slim. I didn't give her no hundred and forty dollars. I feel like we stole from her."

"Gave her seventy, didn't you?"

Amy nodded.

Slim's long, bony face split into a broad grin. "She promised to double your money, didn't she?"

"Yes."

"Didn't keep her promise, did she?"

"No!"

Slim began to laugh. "Next time you want to double an investment, don't you go to no gypsies," he said. "Just come to me!"

For an instant Amy stared at him, and then she too began to laugh. She laughed until she cried. All the way home to Cowboy Rest, Slim and Amy laughed, while their children slept contentedly in the back, bedded on the fanciest supply of groceries the Maines had ever laid in for the winter.

But driving away on Highway Fifty there was no laughter among the gypsies. When they reached the summit of the Austin Grade, they stopped to let the boiling radiator of their tired car cool off. And while they waited, they got out and looked down on the quiet little town of Austin, nestled below them in Pony Canyon.

The tall gypsy woman, her eyes blazing in the haggard beauty of her face, shook a clenched fist as she stood on the mountain top, and swore, "We won't set foot in that place again. Not us, nor any of our peole. We gypsies have a new name for Austin. We call it Double Trouble!"

The gypsies turned south on 8A at the Frontier Tavern, headed toward greener pastures in Tonopah and Las Vegas. And to this day, they have kept their word. They never come to Austin anymore.

A Day on the Mountain with the Basque Buckaroos

118 WHEN I CAME TO CENTRAL NEVADA I was intrigued to find Basques all over the state. In Nevada there are Basque restau-

rants, Basque bars, Basque casinos, and Basque hotels; there are Basque lawyers, Basque clergy, Basque politicians, Basque university professors, Basque journalists, Basque authors, and Basque livestock operators. These ancient and mysterious people had fascinated me during my childhood when I visited the *Pays Basques,* in the Pyrenees Mountains between France and Spain. To find them again was a wonderful surprise.

Traditionally rural Basques are associated with sheep-tending. Not only were there Basque sheep outfits neighboring us, but for several years my husband leased grazing rights on some of his Grass Valley Ranch range to a sheep man, and we were in constant contact with his herders. I speak French, and because many of the young herders were freshly arrived in Nevada from the Old Country and knew no English, I was often called in to act as an interpreter for the French Basques. With the Spanish Basques I was unable to be of assistance as I speak no Spanish.

119

Even more interesting to me than my contact with the Basque shepherds, was to find Basque buckaroos in Nevada. Nothing in the Basque cultural heritage suggests cowboying as a vocation, but circumstances alter cases. Many of the buckaroos on the Central Nevada cattle ranches were Basques. More than with the sheepherders, it was with the buckaroos my associations were closest. And the buckaroos needed no interpreter.

All of them had lived many years in Nevada. They spoke their own oddly accented brand of American, rolling their r's and adding musically unconventional syllables to the language. My ranch work threw me together with them because I too had adapted to life in the Far West and did a good deal of the cowboying with my husband's cattle.

The Basque buckaroos were all fine men. They were loyal, hardworking, courageous, lighthearted, and kind. I remember every one of them with affection. But I must admit as buckaroos, with one or two exceptions, they were out of their proper element and quite obviously would have been happier afoot than on horseback.

Originally the Basques who worked as buckaroos had come to America to tend sheep. In many instances the rancher for whom they worked was also Basque and had often been instrumental in bringing them to this country. He might even be a close relative or have come from the same small village in the Pyrenees. It was not surprising then that most of these men stayed a lifetime with the same outfit, often on a partnership basis. This was how it came about that when on some ranches cows replaced sheep as a more profitable operation, shepherds were transformed into buckaroos. When this happened, they brought to their new occupation interpretations of the art of cowboying which were uniquely their own.

Cowboying on the Grass Valley Ranch was normally a sedate and uneventful business. But when the Basque buckaroos rode over the mountain from Reese River, the primeval silences of the valley were shattered. The canyons rang and rang again with shouts and imprecations and thundering hoofs that carried undertones of tribal warfare reminiscent of the Battle of Roncevaux.

These Basque rides were an annual event in the years before fences were built by the Bureau of Land Management to
divide the ranges and stop the seasonal drift. When there
were no fences, there would be a summer-long mingling of
herds in the high country, until the golden days of late summer when the cattle grazing in common on the mountains of
Cental Nevada began to seek the lower levels in anticipation
of the dark winter months ahead.

As the cattle started moving out of the mountains, not all
the cows would return to their respective home ranges of
their own accord. And so it was customary in autumn for the
ranchers to send their buckaroos to ride the neighboring
ranges and gather their strayed cows.

One day in particular stands out in my memory. It was the
last communal ride before the drift fence was built along the
top of the Toiyabe Mountains between Reese River and Grass
Valley, the last ride before such rides were to become only
history. To me this final ride seemed to epitomize everything
that was fierce and gay and quixotic about my old friends, the
Basque buckaroos.

The buckaroos converged upon Grass Valley on an October evening to camp a few miles above our ranch house in one
of our fields which lies beside Skull Creek where huge cottonwoods, covered with leaves like gold medallions, unfurl their
branches above the rushing waters.

Some came in high, rickety ranch trucks, bedrolls and
horses piled pell-mell in the back, rattling down the Long
Ridge from Austin on the dusty Grass Valley road. And the
Silver Creek riders, led by Philip Guerrano, packed over the
Skull Creek Pass, their driven horses leaving a long, low-
hanging dust cloud above the canyon.

Philip usually rode a raw-boned roan gelding and dragged
behind him, by means of a rope halter, a rusty black. I suppose
the black was intended for use if the roan gave out, which
seemed most unlikely for he was as lean and iron sinewed as
Philip himself.

Between horse and rider existed a distrust born of numerous mutual betrayals. The roan took sardonic delight in waiting for Philip to start to dismount. As Philip cautiously freed **121**

his foot from the stirrup, the roan would erupt into a series of formidable bucks. Philip would catapult from the saddle to land ignominiously on his head. All of us except Philip found this uproariously funny. But Philip made great efforts to out-maneuver the roan, spurring him into a wide-open gallop, then snatching him up short before he could collect himself to buck. Dismounting was the only time Philip was ever known to go faster than a trot. He trotted his roan from dawn until dark, and then, because he had a complete disregard for time, from dark until dawn.

At the sight of Philip approaching at a purposeful trot, supposedly domesticated cows became imbued with the ferocity of Spanish fighting bulls and the cunning of aurochs. Those cows which failed to charge him head-on took to the hills, lurking in tangles of junipers, and even circling around behind to stalk him warily as he sought to flush them out of hiding.

More than anyone I have known, the sight of Philip on his raw-boned roan reminded me of Don Quixote.

When I drove the jeep up to the buckaroo camp at Skull Creek after supper to see if there was anything needed that I could bring to them, the first man to greet me, shouting welcome, was Philip. Beside him stood a little round man, a stranger to me, who looked like Sancho Panza. He was arrest-ingly dressed in heavy, grey woolen golf stockings pulled up over the outside of his Levi legs, and his beret was jammed down over his ears like a bucket. Philip introduced Sancho Panza as, "My helper, Fermin."

After greeting them and the others, I walked toward the black, patched tents which were humped in a semicircle under the giant trees. Near them, over an open fire, Black Pete was cooking. As I approached he lifted the lid from a cast-iron pot, and appetizing smells of simmering mutton stew, garlic, wood smoke and boiling coffee swirled toward me. A round, hard-crusted loaf of camp-made sourdough Basque bread lay by the fire alongside a jug of red wine. "You stay for supper?" Black Pete invited. His invitation pleased me, for I could remember a time when Black Pete would not even ride with me because he considered it unseemly to ride after cattle with a woman. But during the years I was usually the only one riding for Grass Valley Ranch, and if Pete wanted to ride my husband's range he sooner or later was forced to ride with me.

Black Pete used to tell me about those remote, lawless years when he first came to Nevada from the Old Country and went to work herding sheep for the Grass Valley Ranch. Those were the days when twenty-two thousand sheep headquartered at Grass Valley and ranged in trespass from the lush meadowlands of the Humboldt River to the parched deserts south of Tonopah.

I loved to hear how, long before I was born, Black Pete tramped these hills and fought and fled for his life from the cattle ranchers warring to protect their range rights. But this evening I did not linger at the camp to talk. I knew the Basques were anxious to get settled, and so I paused only long enough to greet Buckaroo Joe.

Buckaroo Joe was a stocky, heavy-set man who radiated an air of quiet competence. He was cow boss for Walt Whitaker, a Fallon rancher who owned ranches in Reese River. Joe was an old friend of Black Pete's and Philip's, though a comparative stranger to me. But I was shortly to know him a good deal better.

Night was falling when I reached the house. Before going inside, I paused to look back up Skull Creek where I could see the warm light of the camp fire shining through the dark. It was the only light visible, aside from those of the ranch, for miles in every direction.

For three or four days after they got to Grass Valley the Basques were busy gathering their cattle. Finally they had the big end of them held under fence in the Skull Creek field.

Early on the morning of the day they planned to drive their cows back over the mountain to the Reese River side, I rode up to join them. It was my intention to go with them to the limit of the Grass Valley Ranch range boundary on the top of Skull Creek Pass, to assure that none of my husband's cows went over the mountain with them.

123

When I arrived, the cattle were already bunched at the upper end of the field below a sheer rock cliff. Along the top of this perpendicular cliff raced a cow, furiously followed by a rider on a faded buckskin horse. From below I recognized the rider as the Sancho Panza-like Fermin. The cow was one of my husband's elderly purebred Herefords whom I had never before seen travel at a gait faster than a stately waddle.

"That's my cow!" I cried. "Why is that idiot chasing her?"

Beside me old Philip shrugged narrow shoulders. "Because she has horns," he said. "Fermin thinks she is a bull."

"Can't he read her brand?"

Philip's long thin face wrinkled into a disarming grin. "What do brands mean to Fermin? He can't read them!"

I gave a gasp as over the face of the cliff plummeted the cow. Then, my eyes were wrenched from her falling body by the nightmare spectacle of Fermin passionately urging his lemon-yellow charger over the cliff behind her.

"Stop him! He'll be killed!"

The grin had not left Philip's face. It broadened. "Killed?" he laughed. "He doesn't know enough to get killed!"

In an avalanche of sliding rock they—cow, horse, and Fermin, all miraculously unhurt—reached level ground together.

"Fermin is new to the cattle," Philip explained. "He has been all his life with the sheep. But I am training him to take my place."

"Surely you aren't planning on leaving Silver Creek!" I said incredulously. For years, through good times and bad, old Philip had worked at Silver Creek for John Laborde, a fellow Basque.

Philip's hunched, gothic shoulders, hooded eyes, ugly, humorous face, long chin half hidden in a high, knotted muffler that blew behind him like a banner cloud, was immutable as the hills he rode over. But there had been too many spills off the raw-boned roan, too many broken bones, too many long hours spent under blazing suns and bitter winds chasing recalcitrant cows.

124

"I'm going to retire," Philip said. "I'm getting old." His eyes strayed briefly to Black Pete who was riding toward us. "That one too," he said, "should stop while he can. This is no life for us old ones."

But Black Pete did not show his years as with blazing eyes he cried, "Hold the cows! We must go back and look through the field again. My bull is missing!"

"What bull?" snarled Philip, anxious to get going.

"I bring him from Ox Corral yesterday. That bull! He is the smart one. He want to stay in Ox Corral. All day I bring him, and now—where is he!"

It was not impossible that the bull had crawled through the Skull Creek fence and returned to his favorite nook in Ox Corral. Ox Corral lies eight or nine miles south of Skull Creek, and the distance would have been nothing to a determined animal. But it seemed more probable that he was hiding in the field.

We beat the willows hunting for Pete's bull along the creek banks. We thumped through quaking aspens. I sent my dogs to look and look again. No bull.

As bulls grow old they lose that gregariousness which characterizes young bulls. They become solitary and contemplative. And they have an uncanny ability to hide. Standing absolutely immobile in the shade of a few willows they blend into the surrounding country, camouflaged from all but the most penetrating eye. It seemed only too likely that Pete's bull had done this, and sure enough, when I was riding home that evening, the first thing I saw when I rode into the Skull Creek field was Pete's bull, peering out at me like Pan from the willows.

But that morning, time was pressing, and we were forced to give up the search. "That sonofagun—" said Pete. "He go back to Ox Corral!"

"Then we start?" asked Buckaroo Joe impatiently, trotting up and reining his fat pinto gelding to the gate and dragging it open.

Buckaroo Joe had been with Whitaker thirty years, and the six thousand head that carried Whitaker's T5 brand were

125

Buckaroo Joe's responsibility and pride. Joe had a man with him, the only rider that day except myself who was not Basque. He was a loud-voiced Texan and rode a willing, roman-nosed sorrel with a bald face. I felt sorry for his horse as the Texan doubled and drove him unceasingly after stragglers, but I should have saved my sympathy. The horse could take care of himself, as the day's events would prove.

We had left the field.

Lined out in front of us were around a hundred and fifty head of cattle, going quietly up the canyon. I had dropped far back, talking with Philip. Just ahead of us rode Black Pete.

Pete sat a horse as though he belonged in the saddle. Dressed in dark, drab, work-worn chaps and Levi's, a wisp of bright silk tied tight at his throat, he made a gallant figure. His face was hard, the features stern and fierce, yet an underlying quality of gaiety gave him an expression of great charm. No longer young, Pete's back was straight as a boy's. He held his head high, and a battered, broad-brimmed felt hat was pulled low over his piercing grey eyes.

With his magnificent, swashbuckling look, it was a joy to watch him. He made me think of desperate tales of smuggling along the French-Spanish border when just such bold, dark, daring men as he slipped quietly over the frontier on moonless nights. But this was no moonless night. A luminous sun streamed from a bare, blue sky. The air tingled. Late October flowers blazed purple and gold. Black Pete threw back his head and, sharp and sweet, whistled a tune.

Then at the Big Spring trouble started.

The Big Spring is a green, deceitful bog along whose borders cows skirt cautiously. But the acolyte Fermin and the rowdy Texan knew nothing of the intricacies of getting around the bog. They pressed the leaders squarely into the center of it. With sinister, sucking sounds the cows mired in the bottomless mud.

The Texan quickly pulled back out of it, but poor Fermin saw only that his precious cows were in trouble. Brave with the reckless courage of total ignorance, he plunged forward to save them. In an instant he and his trusty buckskin were stuck worse than the cows.

Awestruck, I watched the plunging, struggling animals, heard Fermin's plaintive cries for help and wondered how we would ever extricate them. But Buckaroo Joe wasted no time in idle speculation. Taking down his rope, he spurred his big pinto ahead. A deep gully separated him from the point of vantage he wished to reach and from which he hoped to rope and pull out a Whitaker cow. Philip had already thrown a rope to Fermin and was hauling him hand over hand to safety.

Fearlessly Buckaroo Joe headed the pinto at the gully. Equally fearless, the pinto leaped into the empty air. His forefeet touched the far bank and slipped on the greasy surface. Inexorably he fell back into the ravine and disappeared from sight.

Black Pete and I craned from the top of the bank. Far below we could make out the prostrate pinto, belly up. Of Buckaroo Joe there was no sign.

"How can we get Joe out?" I asked Black Pete.

"Why try?" retorted Pete logically. "He must be dead. We push in the bank and bury him here."

"The horse too?"

After an instant's reflection, "We bury the horse with him," decided Pete.

But the pinto had no intention of being buried. With a mighty effort he heaved himself upright and floundered out of his proposed grave. From beneath him popped Buckaroo Joe. Blood streamed from his nose and one finger was bent at an extraordinary angle.

Stolidly Black Pete watched Joe clamber up the bank. Not until Joe stood beside him did he say offhand, "I thought you were dead." Joe shook his head and blood sprayed in all directions. "I heard you!" he amiably accused us. "You don't bury me today, Pete!—at least, not in this ditch! Catch me my horse."

"Don't try to get on, Joe," I protested. "I'll ride to the ranch and bring the jeep. You have had a terrible fall. Your nose— your finger—maybe other injuries—"

127

"I'll be all right," said Joe, tugging at his dislocated finger. And when Black Pete led up his pinto, he crawled into the saddle and sat mopping blood off his face with a bandana. The mired cows had all managed to struggle through the bog to safety. Shaken, caked with mud, we resumed the slow climb up the mountain.

It was lovely in the high canyon. All shades of gold were in the groves of quaking aspens. Once again Pete burst into his melodious whistling and Buckaroo Joe, bloody but unbowed, joined him. The Texan yelled and cursed as he forced stragglers to keep up with the bunch, but the rest of us rode peacefully, letting the cows set their own pace up the steep trail. At last we reached the summit, the last cow and calf went over the top and began the long descent into Iowa Canyon which would lead them to Reese River Valley. It was time for me to turn back.

From the head of the pass, with my horse standing quietly and my dogs lying at his feet, I watched the Reese River riders start downward.

At that moment the long-suffering roman-nosed sorrel the Texan was riding bogged his head between his knees, let loose a bellow and lit off down the mountain in a crescendo of spine-cracking bucks. The Texan's head collided with the sorrel's. His nose flattened on his face. Once more the air was crimson with droplets of bright blood.

Thud! The Texan hit the ground.

Still bucking, the sorrel caromed into the other horses and they began to buck too. Old Philip's roan sunfished down the slope, and the rusty black pulled loose and went crow-hopping off in the opposite direction. Fermin's buckskin bolted. The pack horses scattered to the four winds, taking the cows with them.

With cries of fury, Black Pete rounded on plunging horses and stampeding cows. My eyes met Buckaroo Joe's, and simultaneously we began to laugh. Joe's nose was swollen big as a potato, but he could still laugh. Together, we laughed and laughed. And then I turned regretfully away and, followed by my dogs, headed down the empty canyon.

128

The Basque buckaroos are gone from Grass Valley. Philip has retired. Buckaroo Joe has moved away. Fermin has gone back to the sheep. Black Pete is dead. Only the memory of their shouting and their music, their bloodshed and their fury and their tremendous laughter lingers, like a smile on the face of the old mountain.

Mount Callaghan

FLYING OUT OF RENO the air was thick with fog. Like a tired bird the plane lurched slowly upward, and wisps of cloud snatched at its heavy wings.

There was no world for us to see outside the giant plane. Fog was above and below us. The hum of the motors soothed our ears, and soon all of us were reading.

A watery ray of sunlight across the pages of my book made me glance out the window. There, in all its beloved beauty, was a sight which caught the breath in my throat and brought quick tears to my eyes. Diagonally across the window stretched the snow-covered range of the Toiyabe Mountains. In the foreground, framed by the window, rose the smooth bulk of Mount Callaghan.

Toiyabe is a Shoshone word. Translated literally it means "big mountain." *Toi* big, *ya-be* "mountain."

The Toiyabe Range is—as mountains go—of comparatively recent date. Its outlines are jagged. Time has not worn the proud crags and precipices of Arc Dome, Bunker Hill, Toiyabe Peak, and the lesser mountains of the range.

Only Mount Callaghan, at the northern extremity of the range, looms like a relic of an earlier age. Its contours are smoothed by countless years. Its heart is a hollowed crater, **129** left by some long-vanished glacier which once crouched on its very summit.

The Indians tell strange tales of the old mountain. High on its slopes wells a magic spring, invisible to all save the initiated. Along its canyons have been seen waves of blue snakes, overpowering in their evil odor, and so swift and numerous that they cover the earth like the sea, and vanish in an instant. Up Skull Creek—where once was fought a fearful battle in which were slain many warriors—is the doorway to the Shoshone Hell. On dark nights the door gapes wide; souls of departed Shoshones wail with the wind over the high passes of Mount Callaghan.

I leaned forward in my seat, keeping Mount Callaghan in view as long as possible. Inexorably the plane left it further and further behind, until it slipped away over the horizon.

130